VISITING THE SICK

Patti Normile

VISITING THE SICK
A Guide for Parish Ministers

ST. ANTHONY MESSENGER PRESS

CINCINNATI, OHIO

Nihil Obstat: Rev. Nicholas Lohkamp, O.F.M.
Rev. Robert L. Hagedorn

Imprimi Potest: Rev. John Bok, O.F.M.
Provincial

Imprimatur: +James H. Garland, V.G.
Archdiocese of Cincinnati
November 27, 1991

The *nihil obstat* and *imprimatur* are a declaration that a book is considered to be free from doctrinal or moral error. It is not implied that those who have granted the *nihil obstat* and *imprimatur* agree with the contents, opinions or statements expressed.

Cover design and photography by Don Nesbitt
Book design by Julie Lonneman

ISBN 0-86716-150-7

Published by St. Anthony Messenger Press
Printed in the U.S.A.

Contents

Introduction

The lobby of the hospital where I have worked for a number of years both as a volunteer and as an employee is adorned with a life-size mural of the pool at Bethesda (see John 5:1-15). I often think as I walk past this depiction of physical cures how I would love to escort patients to the edge of the pool. I would hold their arms as they walked into the water or, with the help of a friend, lower them into waters rippled by angel wings. They would, of course, step from the pool, waters cascading from their bodies, cured of all illness of body, mind and spirit, praising the God who had cured them.

But cures do not always happen that way. Cures themselves are often long and difficult procedures. And some people are never cured. Chronic illnesses reshape the lives of those who struggle with their diseases year after year. Accidents, disease and death can strike swiftly and without warning. Cures of physical symptoms and their causes are not always possible.

Healing is. Healing comes to the person who discovers her worth even when incapacitated. Healing comforts the individual who knows that death is approaching but believes that the God who created him will redeem him. Healing emerges from the suffering and humiliation of illness when a patient realizes that these difficulties have revealed a strong spiritual person.

While we cannot lead patients into the pool of Bethesda, we can lead them to God's healing through the ministry of pastoral care. This book is intended for the people in that ministry: those who serve as pastoral caregivers or eucharistic ministers in hospitals, homes or nursing homes.

It begins with an exploration of the ministry itself in Chapter One—its "theology," if you will. Chapter Two will help you prepare for visiting the sick or homebound. Chapter Three offers practical advice which, although it applies largely to any visit to the sick, focuses on visiting patients in the hospital. Chapter Four considers the distinctive aspects of a visit in a home or a nursing home. Chapter Five explores caring for the caregivers— yourself included. And Chapter Six offers an assortment of prayers and blessings for use in your ministry. Other Resources, the listing at the end of the book, suggests directions for continuing growth in your ministry.

Pastoral care of the sick is a "Christmas ministry." Our mission is to bring to patients the awareness that Christ—Emmanuel, God with us—is born anew within us. Through our visits we hope to be instruments of light and hope breaking through the darkness of doubt and despair.

CHAPTER ONE

Ministry to the Sick and Dying

In writing this book I began at the end: with praying, writing and gathering the prayers that are included in Chapter Six. Ministry to the sick and the dying always begins with prayer. There is no other starting place. Authentic ministry begins with prayer—that special connectedness with God—or it is not Christian ministry. Minus prayer, it becomes some other activity which may have value. But God is the source, the only source, of our ministries. As Christians, we acknowledge Jesus as the channel through which our ministries flow.

My own ministry to the sick stems from my inability to visit Dick, a lifelong friend who suffered from multiple sclerosis. I wanted to visit, but did so too rarely and only for brief times. I did not know how to be present to a once-vital person who was ultimately unable even to scratch his own nose. His disease-caused disability left me disabled as a friend.

Throughout my life I also have observed my parents' personal ministries to the sick and bereaved. Mom and Dad probably wouldn't call what they do "ministry"; to them it is just doing what needs to be done—praying for and taking care of those in need. (Perhaps that is the most perfect kind of ministry: a ministering life.) It took quite a chunk of my lifetime for the goodness of my parents' outreach to those who struggle with illness or disability to reach my consciousness. When it did, I knew I wanted to follow the way they had led.

Though we do not enter pastoral care of the sick just to feel good about ourselves, the personal benefits are inescapable. A ten-year study done by the University of Michigan Survey Research Center and supported by other research groups revealed in 1988 that people who participate in regular volunteer work experience dramatically longer life expectancies. It is fair to add that the quality of those extended lives is enhanced by outreach to those in need.

We volunteer for pastoral ministry because we are needed. Current pressures heighten the need. Hospital nursing staffs, faced with high staff-patient ratios, have less time to provide emotional and spiritual support for their patients. Escalating hospital costs cause hospital administrators to curtail budgets in areas they believe have less direct affect on patient well-being, and pastoral care falls under the budgetary scalpel. The number of ordained clergy is diminishing. Pastors who are responsible for all of the details of parish or congregation ministry may have difficulty carving hospital and nursing home time from their exhausting schedules.

This decrease in availability of pastoral care comes at a time when its value is more broadly recognized. *You* are needed in hospitals and nursing homes! And this book is intended to help you.

Pastoral Identity

Who are we as we knock on a hospital room door? Who are we as we seek a patient in a nursing home lounge? What authority sends us to the parents of a stillborn child or the family of an auto accident victim? How do we identify ourselves?

We come as Christians. Our call to ministry threads through the Scriptures:

> Then the king will say to those on his right, "Come, you who are blessed by my Father. Inherit the kingdom prepared for you from the foundation of the world. For I was hungry and you gave me food, I was thirsty and you gave me drink, a stranger and you welcomed me, naked and you clothed me, ill and you cared for me, in prison and you visited me." Then the righteous will answer him and say, "Lord, when was it that we saw you...?" And the king will say to them in reply, "Amen, I say to you, whatever you did for one of these least brothers of mine, you did for me." (Matthew 25:34-37a, 40)

In Jesus' travels in the Galilean countryside he healed the blind, the deaf, those afflicted with paralysis and mental disorders, hemorrhage and leprosy. Clearly the sick claimed high priority in Jesus' care.

Miracles—that is what we call Jesus' healing of the afflicted. His earthly work of healing astonishes us as it did those who witnessed his healing touch two thousand years ago. As Jesus prepared to leave his earthly ministry in the hands of those who followed him, he reminded them, "Amen, amen, I say to you, whoever believes in me will do the works that I do, and will do greater ones than these, because I am going to the Father" (John 14:12). We are called to be miracle-workers. The miracle we work is bringing the assurance of God's love to those who suffer.

Our original call to minister to God's people flows from our Baptism. Baptism is our *christ*ening, the sacrament of Christ-in-us. Some answer this call through ordained ministry; others reach out in Christ's name as laity. Ordained and lay, together we are the Body of Christ. We walk among the hurting and the hopeless of our day to do as the French proverb says: "to heal sometimes, to remedy often, to comfort always." Those of us who are called to pastoral care of the sick are not invited as limited human beings. We are the embodiment of Christ empowered by the Holy Spirit. We come not as individuals in a one-to-one undertaking but as members of an entire body of believers whose prayer supports our ministry. Ours is a mission, a sending forth, to those who bear the burden of damaged bodies, minds and spirits.

Laypeople do not go *in place of* priests, brothers and religious sisters. They enter this ministry in their own right:

> From the fact of their union with Christ the head flows the laymen's right and duty with respect to be apostles. Inserted as they are in the Mystical Body of Christ by baptism and strengthened by the power of the Holy Spirit in confirmation, it is by the Lord himself that they are assigned to the apostolate. If they are consecrated a kingly priesthood and a holy nation (see 1 Peter 2:4-10), it

is in order that they may in all their actions offer spiritual sacrifices and bear witness to Christ all the world over. (*Decree on the Apostolate of the Laity*, #3)

"You go too....The call is addressed to everyone: laypeople as well are personally called by the Lord, from whom they receive a mission on behalf of the Church and the world." (Pope John Paul II, *The Vocation and Mission of the Lay Faithful in the Church and in the World*, #2)

In its finest form pastoral care is a meld of ordained and lay ministers. Jesus says to all of us, "As the Father has sent me, so I send you" (John 20:21b). Together we possess gifts of compassion, understanding, wisdom, peace and comfort to offer the sick. The gifts we offer glow with the spark of the Holy Spirit dwelling within us.

The Call to Ministry to the Sick

If you are a parish priest or pastoral associate whose job description includes visiting the sick, you may have little choice in entering this ministry. If you choose to be a volunteer visitor or eucharistic minister in a hospital or nursing home, particular motivations have led you to this point. In either case, it is important to assess and confirm your call to this ministry.

Reasons for undertaking a ministry of pastoral care to the sick are as varied as the individuals who enter this work. Sarah's mother suffered from Alzheimer's disease for six years before her death. Sarah grew in understanding of the needs of the families and staff who care for patients with Alzheimer's. She has chosen a nursing home ministry as a way to share the knowledge she has gained.

Father John's assignment to St. Ann's Church requires him to visit the sick as part of his parish responsibilities. He is not totally comfortable in this role but eager to learn. He realizes part of his learning experience will be dealing with the memory of his brother's sudden death in a hospital when they were children.

Though our personal calls to ministry may come through our life experiences, our goals must always be for the benefit of the patients, not to meet our own needs.

Recognizing my inability to face illness and disability in a dear friend, I searched for a way to confront my fear of sickness and hospitalization. A practicum experience in a lay pastoral ministry program offered me a way into the hospital. Under the guidance of a skilled chaplain, I was challenged to confront my own issues while helping others deal with their hospitalization. The experience was so fulfilling that, although I had committed for one hundred hours, I stayed for years and pursued further professional training.

What happened during those mentored hours that changed my perspective and turned a failing into a calling? Patients taught me the meaning of the word *patient*. I learned that as an impatient person I had no tolerance for sickness. Always living and planning for tomorrow diminishes today. Patients are compelled to live today. They have little choice. They contend with today's pain and treasure today's hope. To celebrate with patients on those days of hope, to comfort them on the days when life scares them nearly to death is a privileged blessing.

Pastoral care helps patients be patient and hopeful in the only time any of us have to live—now. Those who live with hope heal faster and live longer.

Confirming the Call

A trusted individual—a spiritual director, hospital chaplain, pastor or mentor—can enable you to reflect upon your call. Is it actually what you are called to do at this time of life? Seeking suggestions about the background and training required may help you determine if you are called to this ministry. As you confirm your call through prayer, be alert to the nudgings of the Spirit who directs you.

Challenge your call to ministry by reflecting on how experiences of illness or injury have affected your life. Consider how you have grown spiritually through these experiences. Life issues can be stumbling blocks to ministry if not addressed. When acknowledged and dealt with, these issues become stepping stones toward those who suffer.

Be willing to consider seriously what issues in your own life will affect your ministry positively or negatively. Chronic illness in your family can either bring compassion or foster frustration. Caring for your aging parents can either make you understanding or create anxiety in dealing with the elderly.

Resisting your own mortality can make you uneasy

with those on the threshold of death. Once you have faced your fear of death, you can more deeply cherish your immortal potential. You are then free to share the perspective of those who encounter death.

Ask yourself these questions to test your call to ministry to the sick, the suffering and the dying:

- What is my personal experience of illness, suffering and death?
- Where is God in that experience?
- Who am I? Do I know myself intimately?
- Why am I seeking this ministry now?
- What do I hope to gain? What do I hope to give in this ministry?
- What do I expect to learn from this experience?
- Who will guide me and support me in this ministry?

An Opportunity for Growth

If you choose a ministry of pastoral care of the sick, you will find that growth is inherent in the work. The sick themselves will teach you about the circumstances they are forced to face. They will tell you of the victories (the former tennis player who succeeded in taking one step in therapy). They will teach you about their diseases (Gary, who taught me a wealth of information about AIDS; Debra, who battles the pain of sickle cell by telling those who will listen what it is like to fear passing an inescapable disease on to her children). The patients will heighten the value you place on each day of life (Mark, whose brain cancer was consuming a mind that had been part of his corporation's "think tank" of brilliant young executives, continually devised new systems to remember important knowledge that he felt slipping from his mental grasp).

If you are uncomfortable with tears, you will find yourself crying at the gentleness of a young couple who have lost a baby. If you shed tears easily, you may find yourself developing a new courage when you know your patient cannot bear to see your tears. If you are afraid of death, you will come to see it as a blessing to some who are too tired to continue living. If you are afraid of life, you will gain courage from those who have little hope yet challenge life for all it will yield to them. If you have a queasy stomach, you will discover your fortitude when a young motorcycle accident victim shows you where his hip hit the highway. If you are a talker, you will learn to treasure silence. If you are quiet, you will speak with wisdom. Pastoral care of the sick will shower you with opportunities for growth.

Some growth will be accidental. Experience will teach you what you did not know you were lacking. Other learning must be intentional. You must seek to develop what is difficult for you. Experiences will demand that you seek to understand them.

Journaling is a valuable tool for the pastoral care provider. As you record the day's visits and their impact on you, you will gain understanding of yourself. As you look back at these entries months after the date of writing, you will rejoice in the development you see in yourself as a pastoral visitor and as a person.

Write about who and what makes you angry. Record

hidden fears that creep up on you when you are with some patients. Confess to yourself your inadequacies. Talk to yourself about these discoveries. Intense feelings about a patient often reveal something about yourself. Jean's aversion to domineering men led her to counseling where she unraveled childhood abuse. Paula's aversion to overweight women led her to acknowledge her rejection of herself. She joined Overeaters Anonymous and lost eighty pounds and gained the ability comfortably to visit *all* women.

A journal provides a perfect place to record praises of God. Mine often becomes a prayer book. What begins as an account is transformed during the writing into a prayer of praise. You will witness miracles of God's grace and power in the lives of your patients. Some will be miracles of physical healing. You probably will not document them scientifically, but you will remember them as occasions of God's love. Others will be miracles of spiritual healing and reconciliation that transforms lives. Your journal will become your testament of God working in the world today, the acts of an apostle in pastoral care—you!—and a place for your faith to grow.

New cases will prompt you to look for new approaches in ministry. Inquire at your church or hospital pastoral care department regarding reading related to ministry to the sick. A suggested reading list is included at the end of this book.

Seminars, classes and workshops for development of pastoral care skills are available in many towns and cities. Lay pastoral ministry programs offer training in ministerial skills. Hospital pastoral care departments, area seminaries, diocesan offices, parish programs, colleges and universities are sources of information about learning opportunities.

If you desire professional training, clinical pastoral education (CPE) programs offer training under supervision in a variety of settings, including hospitals. This training is usually offered in units of four hundred hours of service; a fee is involved. Your local hospital may be able to provide information regarding CPE programs.

It is important to have access to a competent and trusted individual with whom you can process what is happening in your life. This individual may be a spiritual director with whom you can share the insights gleaned from being present to the sick or struggle with the issues of the dying. Together you can explore the direction your experiences lead you.

Or you may choose a mentor—someone involved in the health-care field or one whose wisdom and knowledge enable and support you as you challenge the issues you uncover within yourself. Support may also come from a hospital chaplain who supervises your work and enables you to discern what you do well and what in your ministry you would like to improve.

If the health care facility where you serve has a group of volunteer pastoral care people, the coordinator of that group may meet occasionally with you to moderate discussions of the group's ministries.

Whomever you select to aid you must be trustworthy with your deepest confidences and must have some knowledge of the ministry you are entering.

The choices for support are many and varied. Do not try to solo in ministry. When you are alone, it is far too easy to crash when you meet with difficult people or situations. A brief conversation with someone familiar with the ministry can bring objectivity and growth. Without that support, burnout is a strong possibility.

Do not allow these cautions to drive you away from ministry to the sick. If you feel called, do it. You are needed. The sick and suffering are at vulnerable points in their lives. They may turn to God—or they may turn away. With a caring person to share with them, they can find a stronger faith. A wise saying claims that to affirm another person is to become cocreator with God of that person. As we visit with the sick, we affirm that they are of infinite worth even though they may be able to do little. We affirm that God loves them in their weakness. Through our ministries we join God in the continuing creation of individuals into the people God would have them become.

The Theology of Pastoral Care

The old-style hospital gown, with its open back and string ties, revealed as much as it concealed. Its design symbolizes the vulnerability shared by most patients. We devote much of life to trying to cover and protect ourselves. We cover our ignorance with education, our fears or anger with smiles, our nakedness with clothing, our faces with beards or makeup, our loneliness with bravado, our inadequacies with pseudo-confidence and sometimes our doubts with religion. Hospitalization, symbolized by the hospital gown, invites the sick to accept the humbling nature of the experience. A

14

humbled human is open to the spiritual journey. The pastoral care provider has the privilege of supporting the patient on that journey.

The underlying question that guides the journey is, "Where is God in these events?" Your task in pastoral care is to be present to patients as they attempt to find God in their life situation, to listen as they grow in awareness and understanding of themselves and their God, to encourage them to grow in faith.

"Theology," stated Anselm of Canterbury, "is faith seeking understanding." As you minister to the sick, you will encounter some who have a tiny little grain of faith like the proverbial mustard seed. Through your ministry you attempt to help them cultivate the ground so that the seed of faith can burst forth and grow. You will also meet people whose faith amazes you. No matter what the scope or maturity of an individual's faith, sickness is an occasion when people search for understanding. Times of sickness have the potential to become periods of spiritual growth.

In *Mirrors of God*, Father Joseph Goetz describes theology as "the act of articulating...what we believe and why we believe *here and now*." He further states that every believer is "meant to be...an *inquiring* Christian prepared to express, *at least for oneself*, the reasons for the faith he or she has within. Thus every Christian is called to *do* theology." Our challenge is to help patients "do" their own theologizing. In that way they will come to recognize God in the experience of sickness and be able to articulate that understanding.

Theologian Karl Rahner, S.J., insisted that humanity is fundamentally directed toward God. Many events in life can distract us from that primary orientation. Sickness can be one of the distractions, but it can also become an arena of openness to God's presence. Whether the sick are angry at God because of their physical condition or seeking God's healing, the vulnerability that sickness introduces into life provides an opportunity for them to redirect their lives toward God.

Being seriously ill or hospitalized is like a journey into a strange land. The language of medicine may be a foreign tongue. Patients may be uncertain about the direction in which they are going. Their diet may be changed. They are not sure when they may return home. In the meantime, they must trust those who are sent to guide their days.

Illness stimulates fear in those whom it invades. Fear of death, fear of impairment, fear of pain, fear of separation from what is loved, known and trusted in life—all spawn when the tide of illness overtakes people. Their lives may seem threatened even by minor ailments as fear grips them.

Peggy kept wiping the tears from her eyes in the hospital waiting room. "I know it's foolish to cry. Megan is only having tubes put in her ears. The boys both had that done several times and they were fine. But she's so little and I can't be with her now. It makes me sad—afraid something might go wrong."

Scripture says, "There is no fear in love, but perfect love drives out fear..." (1 John 4:18a). The goal of pastoral care is to bring the love of Jesus to the individual so that fear may be expressed and begin to abate—so that healing occurs. Diseases are cured; people are healed. A *cure* for an illness may not always be forthcoming, but *healing* is always possible. People can be healed of their fears, their doubts, their guilt, their anger, their loneliness. In that way lives are healed whether or not disease symptoms or the results of age or injury can be erased.

During times of crisis, darkness can overwhelm the light within an individual. The gospel call is to bring light to what is hidden in darkness. *Crisis*, from the Greek *crino*, means a turning point or a breakthrough. Those involved in pastoral care of the sick come to help illuminate the darkness created by a crisis of doubt, fear and uncertainty so that the patient can break through to hope.

You come bringing *shalom* to the sick and the injured. *Shalom* was the gift Jesus spread throughout his earthly ministry. The word signifies more than peace. It indicates wholeness and holiness. Shalom invites each person to live to his or her potential in spite of what ails them physically. Today medical science acknowledges that physical cures are more attainable when spiritual healing has occurred. In *A Kingdom Within*, psychologist John Sanford describes faith as the capacity of a person to affirm life no matter what it may bring. As people of faith we make our experience of faith available to those who need support. We bring shalom.

Your Gifts to the Patient

Someone said that a friend is one who sings us the song of our hearts when we have forgotten the melody. As a pastoral care visitor to the sick, you will come as a spiritual friend to help patients find the notes and words to the songs that their hearts are struggling to sing in the midst of illness or injury.

Christian presence is the essential gift pastoral ministers bring to the sick. Inherent in that presence are three gifts: (1) confidentiality, (2) respect and (3) acceptance. These gifts come wrapped in your personal presence.

1) *Confidentiality*: As a pastoral care visitor, you have access to privileged information. Each patient must be certain that shared information or feelings will be held in strictest confidence. Even the patient's presence in the hospital is confidential unless he or she agrees that you may notify a prayer group or the parish bulletin of the hospitalization. The reason for hospitalization and the patient's condition are likewise confidential. John may not want his hemorrhoids publicized. Miriam's decision to discuss her miscarriage with others is her choice.

2) *Respect* is inherent in any ministry. Each person we approach is God's creation, God's child. The AIDS victim, the drug addict or alcoholic, the unwed mother all deserve from us the respect that reflects God's love for them rather than society's disdain or judgment. Seek the goodness that exists in those whose lives have been shattered by chance or by destructive life-style choices; support them as they begin to build new lives from the pieces. Listen as the young unwed mother considers a job to support herself and her child when they leave the hospital. Review the AIDS victim's life with him,

applauding his accomplishments. Support the chemically dependent individual who realizes that no one else is responsible for harmful behavior. In these roles you become with God cocreators of that human being. From the fragments of broken lives, new lives are molded when individuals see hope and their potential.

3) *Acceptance*: Accept all patients as people in whom God's Spirit lives. Accept them as equals, your brothers and sisters who are part of the Body of which you are a member—the Body of Christ. Accepting them means accepting their anger when you wish them peace; honoring their doubt though it pricks your faith; listening to an account of a brush with death even when it forces you to face your own mortality; valuing their tears and fears as you offer comfort. Only through unconditionally accepting persons can you meet them in the present stage of their journeys and accompany them to a new spiritual place.

Recognizing the Lord

In Luke's Gospel two grieving disciples walk from Jerusalem to Emmaus after Good Friday. They do not at first recognize the stranger who joins them and explains the Scriptures to them. Only when they reach their destination and the stranger breaks bread for them do they recognize the Lord (see Luke 24:13-35). Modern-day parallels of the journey along the road to Emmaus occur in hospital halls and nursing home corridors.

Allen and the parish visitor walked slowly down the

hospital hallway. They talked about the accident that had sent Allen to the hospital several weeks before.

Allen said, "That truck was on us before I could do a thing. No place to go. Helpless, helpless. The next thing I knew people were trying to pry us out of the car. I knew right away...Marilyn...well you know the rest."

George did know the rest; he replied, "You must miss her very much."

Allen readily agreed, "Oh, I do—so much. But, you know, it's strange. In spite of all the hurt and pain, in the last days I've found a kind of peace. You know I've gone to church—well, most of the time. But I never thought much about what I heard there. Tried to live a good life and all of that. But it's beginning to make sense to me—the Resurrection and all. I know Marilyn is gone from this life, but I have this strange feeling that she's very close to me—kind of helping me recover. I have the feeling that she and the Lord are walking with us around this hall."

Allen was experiencing the transformation that his injuries and his wife's death had cast upon him. He was encountering his deepest self, a spiritual self he had not known before. With George as a trusted representative of his Church, Allen is free to talk about this new and healing phenomenon that loss has brought to him.

In pastoral care we attempt to pave new roads to Emmaus for those who struggle to recognize Jesus' presence in the events of their lives. We walk with them, talk with them. Recognition comes as patients unfold their stories to empathetic listeners.

Sympathy Versus Empathy

Sympathy and *empathy* do a lot of word-wrestling these days. *Sympathy* has long meant feeling sorry about another's situation. We regret the person's pain but do not necessarily enter into the experience. *Sympathy* is a word that has lost some muscle. It has come to mean more sentimental emotion than supportive action, more pity than compassion. Sympathy may shroud a hidden agenda as we view another's misfortune ("I'm glad I'm not in your shoes!"). Sympathy puts its arms around a person and moans, "Poor baby!" Sympathy can have a weakening affect. Sympathy is a crutch made of papier-mâché. To the sick it can indicate, "Wow, I really am sick! I won't get well. I'm too weak. Why fight it?"

Empathy in everyday usage is a relatively new kid on the verbal block. It indicates an imaginative leap: To empathize is to move emotionally into another person's skin and from that vantage point attempt to comprehend the level of pain or loss. You can never know exactly what it feels like to be another person. You cannot fully comprehend someone else's experience. For that reason you can never say with complete honesty, "I know how you feel." The patient and the pastoral visitor are unique creations; they experience similar events in different ways because of their individuality.

You can, however, *attempt* to comprehend another's emotional position. That attempt is empathy. Empathy looks the patient in the eye supportively and says, "I hear your fear. Let's look for the strengths you have to overcome it." Empathy empowers others to use sadness, fear or loss as tools to become more than they were before their difficulty.

Compassion is empathy's companion. Derived from Latin, the word literally means "to suffer with." In the New Jerusalem Bible Jesus urges, "Be compassionate just as your Father is compassionate" (Luke 6:36). Jesus has left it to us to do what he did: to be compassionate, to suffer with others and to encourage others to do the same.

When you bring your gift of compassion to the sick, they are no longer alone in their suffering, their anguish, their despair. When you listen to the patients' stories and reflect back to them what you hear them saying, the sharing lightens both the burden and the loneliness of bearing it.

At times even individuals who are extremely close find it difficult to share the burden of pain or fear with each other. They feel that the sharing will place an additional burden on a loved one.

Janet and Walt, for example, had been happily married for thirty-seven years when Walt developed a virulent form of cancer that would claim his life in a few months. As I visited him, we talked about his sadness at leaving Janet. "How is she dealing with this news?" I asked him. "Oh, she doesn't know and I don't want her to! I don't want to worry her!" A long conversation followed concerning their close relationship and the shock that would come as his death approached. We discussed how he had always been honest with her about other matters. He felt this situation was different. Janet was not to know that he was dying.

I later met Janet and we talked about how she felt about Walt's progress. "Oh, I know he is not going to make it," she confessed with sad resignation. "Have you two been able to talk about it?" I ventured. "Oh, no! If he knew that I know how sick he is, he would be so worried about me."

It took several more conversations before Janet and Walt could see that they were living a lie. In the meantime they laughed half-heartedly and made idle conversation because they were afraid to talk about what was really important to both of them. When the wall of deception finally came down, they cried together. Then they began to talk about what really counted: how Janet would be provided for. And they laughed, really laughed at the happy memories. Though they cried at the thought of parting, sharing their knowledge of Walt's illness lightened the burden for both. They lived each day honestly, sharing their lives as they always had done.

You also offer to patients the simple ministry of presence. Sometimes there is no more important gift you can give than sitting at a bedside holding someone's hand. I learned that from Margarite.

Margarite was very old. Her only family was a brother who was also ailing and could not visit her. She had returned to the hospital several times in recent months as her failing heart weakened. "Could you stay awhile and hold my hand?" she asked. "If I can just go to sleep while you're here, I won't be afraid." I did. When I learned that she died the next day, I knew I had been able to provide what she wanted most on her last day.

Presence sometimes seems a costly gift to give. We may have so much to do. But the value of a simple, quiet presence is quite precious.

When you are present to the sick, you are not simply there in your own person. You are there in the person of Christ. His Holy Spirit dwelling within us touches our visits with holiness.

Support for Ministry

We come to the sick as representatives of the Church where we worship. The support of the community is essential to keep ministry from becoming a solo act. We are the Church, the Body of Christ. An elbow by itself can do little good. Joined to an arm which extends from a shoulder to a hand, all activated by an entire system of muscles, nerves and thought, that elbow becomes indispensable.

Sharon is a night nurse in a pediatric hospital. Her work with adolescents in a psychiatric unit is also her ministry. She asked her prayer group to pray for a young girl in her care, identifying her only as "J." J. had said no to drugs until a group of her peers held her down and forcefully injected her. Later, J. tried to avoid them, but the scene was repeated. J. knew nowhere to turn for help. Her family only blamed her. Finally, she was hospitalized when her trauma was noted by a school nurse. Sharon needed the prayer support of her Church as she dealt with the medical and the spiritual needs of J. Two people, Sharon and her patient, received those prayers. One is now a healing teenager; the other avoided professional burnout in a difficult assignment.

Small communities within the larger Church support your ministry. A prayer group may provide spiritual support. A spiritual director or mentor can serve as mediator for the pain you share as you minister to the sick. Your support systems can celebrate with you the triumphs over illness and mourn the times when cures do not occur. Solo ministers are much more likely to burn out and abandon their ministries than are those who have the prayerful support of a worshiping community.

A Member of the Team

Your presence as a pastoral visitor to the sick involves you as a member of the healing *team*. Your efforts to provide for the patient's spiritual concerns contribute to the person's total well-being. People are not sick or hospitalized in fragments. The foot may be the target of bunion surgery, but the whole person is forced to forgo daily activity. When surgery to remove an ovarian tumor is successful and the tumor benign, the patient treasures life a bit more. Your visit may be a time for her to express a new view of her recently threatened life.

As a pastoral care visitor you also come with an advantage: You are not going to *do* something to the patient. No blood tests, X-rays or medications, no probing or examining, no shots are on your agenda. Your visit may serve as a respite from the ongoing regimen of medical care. You are the part of the team that cares for the patient's invisible aspects.

As members of the healing team, pastoral care visitors need to be aware of the ten elements which ensure patient satisfaction noted in a nationwide survey by Press, Ganey Associates, Inc., of South Bend, Indiana (*Michigan Hospitals*, September, 1990):

1) Staff members need to be sensitive to the inconvenience of sickness and hospitalization.

2) Staff must respect patients' privacy.

3) Problems are to be taken seriously.

4) Physicians need to spend time with patients.

5) Cheerfulness is desirable in the hospital.

6) Nurses are to be attentive to patient needs.

7) Nurses responding to patient calls need a positive attitude.

8) Patients want tests explained to them by technicians who administer the tests.

9) Nurses are to provide information on treatments and tests.

10) Hospitals need to be cautious not to discharge patients too soon.

Substitute *visitor* for *staff* or *nurse* to see how important to your ministry many of these points are. Each element of patient satisfaction suggests areas of concern for patients you may be visiting.

Privacy is particularly important to your ministry. Patients have little authority over who comes into their room to provide treatment, tests, food, transportation or therapy. Occasionally patients discover the one area over which they have control: They can ask not to be visited by members of the pastoral care team. This decision is to be respected.

Rod was one who wanted no part of "religious guys

visiting me!" His request was honored—with one small exception. The hospital chaplain always waved, smiled and sent a passing greeting into Rod's room as he went by. This friendly but nonintrusive outreach eventually won Rod over. One day he beckoned the chaplain to come in and talk. The chaplain's patience and respect for Rod's wishes won out.

Without violating confidences, you may want to contact nursing staff or patient representatives in the hospital with pertinent observations about patients. A patient may be reluctant to express a concern to a health-care person but feel free to tell the pastoral care visitor.

Carrie told the nurse that Mr. Adams in 286 was really frightened and thought that the change in treatment meant he was getting worse. The nurse was able to follow up and explain that the alteration in procedure actually meant he had improved. Another pastoral visitor noticed that Thelma's hands seemed quite cold and she was gasping for each breath. The visitor promptly notified a nurse, who discovered that Thelma had pulled her oxygen tube out.

If you work with a hospital chaplain, information you provide about patients can be an invaluable extension of the information he or she gathers personally. Chaplains are committed to preserving confidentiality. Your input continues your ministry to that person after you leave.

The Ultimate Task

Perhaps our ultimate task is to enable patients, shut-ins and nursing home residents to discover the essence of their being. And so I offer my prayer to you:

> Essence is that irreducible fragment of myself.
> Essence exists when all that seems to be me vanishes
>   in a puddle of pain or powerlessness.
> Essence is the infinite spark that empowers my life.
> Essence is the energy that emerges from nothingness
>   and merges with eternity.
> Essence is the communion of self with God.
> Essence is spirit and soul.
> Essence is what I live to create and nurture,
>   yet die in order to possess forever.
> Essence is God living in me and through me.
> Essence transcends the power and the present
>   and permeates a world that will not pass.
> Essence lingers in the love of children, of family,
>   of friends.
> Essence exists when breath waxes and wanes.
> Essence is you, my Lord, in me. Amen.

CHAPTER TWO

Preparing for the Pastoral Visit

T he hospital's computer list indicated that Janice, Room 207, age forty-four, had recently undergone a double mastectomy. I hesitated outside her room, letting my imagination try to creep into Janice's mind. How would she be coping with her loss? Depression and anger were possibilities in a woman relatively young to have such major surgery. Was she fearful for her life? Tears and fears are sometimes teammates. How could I help her deal with her situation?

Taking a deep breath and saying a short prayer—or was it the other way around?—I entered Room 207. Seeing the occupant, I thought perhaps I was in the wrong room. This patient radiated happiness. Tears? Not even close. The merriment in her eyes and her engaging smile were not superficial cover-ups for sadness. Yes, she said, she was Janice.

Janice taught me an invaluable lesson. Never assume a patient's reaction. My imaginary trip into Janice's mind was actually how I imagined *I* would feel in her circumstances.

Janice had just learned that she would be released

from the hospital in time to attend her twin sons' double wedding. She had overcome the first major obstacle that cancer had placed in her life. Sometime Janice would grieve her physical loss. At the time of my visit, however, she wanted to celebrate her victory over cancer's attempt to rob her of a precious event. And celebrate we did in conversation and prayer.

The Purpose of This Visit

Each visit to the sick has its own unique purpose. The visit may be to remind the patient of the parish's concern, to provide encouragement during difficult days, to bring Communion, to pray. Realistically, each visit combines several of the above purposes. The purpose of the initial visit, however, is to assess and, if possible, meet the needs of the patient. My mistake with Janice was to attempt to determine her needs before meeting her.

Gathering information about the patient's condition may be helpful to you in preparing for the visit— providing you do not preconceive the patient's attitude toward the medical facts. Also contact the health-care facility or a family member to determine appropriate visiting hours. Frustration and wasted time result when you arrive as the nurse brings bath water or your patient is being wheeled down the hall to X-ray.

Some visits are requested by the patient; others are initiated by family members, the hospital pastoral care department or parish visitation ministry. Your visit may be anticipated by the patient or may come unannounced.

A visit can be a deep conversation or a brief, casual meeting. Your arrival will sometimes coincide with a time of great need; at other times the patient will have little need of your attention.

In any case, it is the *patient* who sets the tone and direction of a visit. Your encouragement keeps the communication open.

How Are *You* Today?

One Sunday John brought Communion to two hospitalized teenagers. He felt a strange reluctance to enter their rooms. The feeling was so strong after visiting one young man that he was tempted to skip the second teen on his list. Talking with them produced an unnamed anxiety.

Encountering the hospital chaplain later on his rounds, John commented on his resistance to visiting two quite pleasant young people. "How are things going with your kids, John?" the chaplain asked. John instantly recognized the wisdom of the question. His children were at a challenging stage. Just before John left for the hospital that morning, he had discovered a new dent in the car. The two teens unknowingly were telling John that he needed to work on family relationships when he returned home that afternoon.

In preparing for the visit it is important to deal with personal issues in your own life. An argument at home may carry over to your pastoral visit. Acknowledge the incident. Seek whatever reconciliation is possible. Then proceed with the understanding that the event is a factor in your relationships with others at that particular time.

The illness of someone close to you may color your ability to minister. Talking to a newly diagnosed cancer patient may reawaken the pain of watching a loved one struggle with the disease. Awareness that your own experience accompanies you on each visit helps you avoid negative effects. After all, your experience with illness can provide understanding and sensitivity to the patient.

We carry with us on each visit to the sick our own concepts of the meaning of illness and death. One who has had abundant good health may have a different view of illness than one who has experienced frequent bouts of sickness. If you have not acknowledged your own mortality, looking straight in the eye the reality that you will die someday, you may have difficulty empathizing with someone facing death or the threat of death. Discussing such personal issues with a colleague, spiritual guide or mentor will benefit your life's journey as well as the individuals you visit.

The Meaning of Illness and Injury

The stage of life at which an illness or injury strikes a person alters their outlook concerning their convalescence. Marijo, twenty-eight, has three small children and a handsome husband plus youthful strength to inspire her physical rehabilitation after a stroke. John's wife died last year; his children live far away. At eighty-two, he really doesn't know if he wants to improve his speech and recover the motor skills lost as a result of a stroke. Robert was only thirty-two when an industrial accident left him unable to work. He feels guilty that he wasn't more careful, fearful that his wife will not love him as he is, angry that in one brief moment his life changed so dramatically.

Developing an understanding of the issues of the sick and dying is essential to effective ministry. Attitudes toward sickness vary according to whether the illness or condition is permanent, short-term, chronic or involving lengthy recuperation. Accidents can provoke anger or guilt. Blaming another or oneself becomes a major issue. Contagious diseases may discourage or prohibit visitors, creating a sense of loneliness, isolation and abandonment. Despair and loss of hope may afflict those whose prognosis is poor.

The gospel story is about the Word made flesh. Flesh is subject to pain; its highly sophisticated sensory system enables us to learn and to survive. To endure pain and to understand it are physical and mental challenges.

Let's get one thing clear: God does not send pain. The Son was himself subject to pain on earth. Pain is part of being human. It alerts us to potential dangers. It warns when an appendix is ready to rupture or when a cyst invades our abdomens. Dr. Paul Brand, chief of rehabilitation of the National Hansen's Disease Center at Carville, Louisiana, says that if he had one gift to give his patients, it would be the gift of pain. It would warn those patients when they were injuring themselves and thus preserve their flesh from injury.

Yet pain can also paralyze a patient's ability to think, to pray, to function as himself. The more severe the pain, the more difficult the ordinary activities of daily life become. Intense pain creates isolation, since no one is capable of fully understanding another's pain.

Sickness and disability cause other problems in American life. Dropping out of competition during an illness threatens some. The dependency created by sickness shatters the myth of rugged individualism. Hospitalization damages self-esteem in those who pride themselves on self-sufficiency and independence. That damaged self-esteem needs nurturing to enable the patient to reestablish a sense of self-worth. Isolation and loneliness form a cocoon from which the patient may emerge with an increased desire for community or with a sense of rejection.

"Tell me about your work" encourages a patient to discuss a vital area. A patient's room often gives clues to what gives strength. Drawings done in vigorous crayon strokes, reading material on the bedstand—such things provide an excellent launch pad for conversation about what is important, what gives meaning to someone's life. Flowers, cards and balloons (or their absence) speak about the support an individual has.

Mercedes was nearly ninety when she underwent surgery that involved the use of an umbilical cord as replacement tissue. A friend with a matchless sense of humor arrived with a balloon that proclaimed, "It's a boy!" Mercedes' healing was probably hastened by the hearty laughter she enjoyed with each new visitor who enjoyed the irony of the baby balloon in the room of an octogenarian. The balloon also led her to discuss the five baby boys she had reared. They and their families were primary reasons for her to recover from the surgery.

Hospitalized individuals may have deep needs to express a wide range of feelings. Feelings may be masked or quite obvious. Among the most common are:

- anxiety in unfamiliar surroundings;
- longing to go home;
- anger at self, doctor, God, Church, family;
- impatience;
- sadness;
- guilt, self-blame for illness;
- bitterness, resentment;
- loneliness;
- helplessness;
- fear of the economic consequences of illness;
- fear of pain and suffering;
- fear of invalidism;
- fear of separation from loved ones;
- fear of death;
- joy as they reflect on life;
- gratitude at the love of others;
- calm as they adjust to the situation;
- peace as they look to the future;
- deep faith as they trust in God.

Understanding Loss and Grief

Two five-year-old cousins were overheard talking about their feelings regarding a death in their family.

"I don't know why they make such a big deal of it. When you die, you die!"

"And you go to heaven—so what's the big deal?"

"Then why do grown-ups carry on so?"

"It's just a part of it—somethin' they gotta do."

"I guess so, but I wish they wouldn't push us away."

Because these children were not closely associated with the deceased relative, a great-aunt, they did not experience the full grief cycle. They discussed their young assessments of adult behavior. Yet in their innocence, they captured two essential truths about grief: (1) Grief is something we "gotta" do and (2) people need people during periods of grief.

Elizabeth Kubler-Ross, a psychiatrist in Chicago, Illinois, opened an entire new field of understanding with her study of people facing death. She named the five phases of response most individuals experience. The original study involved terminally ill patients, but similar stages of grief accompany other major losses. Different people experience the stages in different ways; the time a person may spend in a particular stage is as varied as individuals themselves.

The importance of understanding the stages of grief is to know that these are *normal* reactions to devastating events. Our job is not to help a grieving person out of a stage but to support that person on the journey through the stages. We do not visit to cheer people up but to enable them to find hope in the situation in which they find themselves.

The brief description of the five stages of grieving that follows is only an introduction; for further reading, see Other Resources on page 139.

Stage One: Denial. The idea of death and catastrophic loss so overwhelms most of us that initially we rebel; we say to ourselves that what is happening is not possible. The doctor must have made a mistake; we'll get another doctor. Think of your past reactions to tragic news. "No, no, no!" is a common response.

Denial provides initial protection from an overwhelming truth. Underneath the denial the individual is hearing the reality of the condition. The facts will surface as the person is able to handle the reality physically, emotionally and psychologically.

Stage Two: Anger. Anger provides an escape valve for the emotions that have built up during the denial stage. Now someone has to be blamed for something beyond the patient's control. A person may seek physical release by punching a pillow (or something more solid like a wall or another person). Resentment and rage may be directed at the doctor for the handling of the case. God may become the scapegoat: "How can you do this to me?" The patient may alienate loved ones if family and friends do not realize that the anger must be expressed. Unfortunately, they are close enough to be targets. Reasoning and arguing with the patient in this stage does little good and may actually prolong the stage. Empathetic listening without judgment is most helpful.

Stage Three: Bargaining. Once anger has subsided, the patient may begin to bargain. The bargaining stage can be an apparently silent time because negotiations may be with God. "If I can just get well, I'll never swear or drink or smoke again." "I'll go to Mass daily if only this surgery is successful."

Stage Four: Depression. Depression is also a silent period of inward movement. The patient may take blame for a life-style—too much working, drinking, smoking, eating; too little exercise, relaxation, compassion for others. Our temptation may be to try removing the feelings of depression. Removal is impossible. Just listening helps. Through conversation, the sorrow inside moves into the light of the outside world. Once underlying feelings are exposed, the patient can take action. A person may seek forgiveness of those wronged or begin to weed out destructive behaviors to replace them with positive actions.

Stage Five: Acceptance. Depending on the cause of grief and/or the physical condition of the person, the fifth stage can be one of quiet, rest, refusal of company. If physical energy is present, however, the person may begin to live according to newfound values. The person may want to share at great length what has been learned from illness or loss. Reconciliation with those who have been estranged may become vital. Sharing memories may bring comfort. At this stage a spiritual companion can be invaluable in reflecting with the individual about the deeper meaning of life.

The stages of grief affect not only the patient but family and close friends as well. They move through the various stages according to the effect of the pending loss and their coping skills. In the process people grieve both what is and what might have been.

Weighing the grief created by the death of an elderly, ailing parent against the grief which wells from the loss of an unborn child is like attempting to compare the value of water and air to human life. Grief is not measurable. Grief cannot be compared, calculated or counted; it must be expressed. The death of an older relative robs us of a known and beloved person whose memory permeates our lives. The loss of an infant deprives us and the world of the potential of a new creation. One wise woman who has experienced her share of life's sorrows states simply, "Grief is grief."

If we are to be helpful companions for others during times of grief related to illness, we must be willing to permit the grieving person to go through these stages of the grieving process. We cannot "should" or "ought" them through the pain: "You *should* talk to your family about your illness"; "you *ought* to be thankful that they found it early." Our presence and our encouragement to share the feelings that surround hospitalization make the time of awaiting emotional and spiritual healing meaningful.

Gary was the first AIDS patient I had met. He was a sensitive, deeply caring guy with many friends who supported and cared for him during his struggle with the disease that would claim his life. He taught me about AIDS. He knew he was passing along valuable information gained from his own inquiries and from his doctors. He helped me past my fear of being with AIDS patients during a period when public knowledge of the disease was often minimal or misleading. That was his gift to me.

My gift to him was one neither one of us understood. We would talk for a while. Then his tears would come. It happened on every visit. Shortly before his death, Gary told me, "I don't understand it. I only cry when I'm with you." I realized I had been granted an enormous compliment. I still treasure his entrusting me with his tears. For some reason I was blessed to be the one with whom Gary could cry.

Valid pastoral care honors patients where they are in the grief process. It does not push them to the place we wish they were. The present has a pressing urgency. Thoughts of a perfectly healthy baby she may have in the future will not wipe away today's pain for the mother of a stillborn. She cannot be comforted by the fact that she has given birth in the past to two beautiful children whom she loves dearly. Her pain is in loss *now*.

'Prayer-Peration' for the Visit

Prayer is an essential initial step in preparing for a visit to the sick. It joins us anew to the Power who brings meaning to this visit—indeed, to life. It focuses on God and the patient rather than on ourselves. In prayer we can shape an image of the patient being loved and cared for by the healing Jesus.

Prayer heals our own dis-eases, whatever they may be. Our dis-ease can be as communicable as our sense of peace and calm. Prayer enables forgiveness of those who disturb our lives; it restores our peace of mind. Prayer enables us to follow Mother Teresa's admonition to begin by making whatever we do something beautiful for God.

CHAPTER THREE

The Pastoral Visit

Each individual, sick or healthy, needs hope for the day. Hope springs up in varied places. It can emerge from anger or sadness or even its antithesis, hopelessness.

What does hope look like? Hope is a sunrise with radiant rays reaching toward today. If you prefer sunsets, hope may be a sunset with all of the promise of the sun's encore tomorrow. Hope embraces you like a mother sending you off to college; she longs to keep you close yet launches you into your own orbit. Hope feels as warm and soft as puppy bellies. Hope has the turning power to alter the direction of our lives like that of a tulip planted upside down. Hope fogs your rear vision mirrors while turning on your headlights.

What does hope look like to a hospital patient? In *I Want to Grow Hair, I Want to Grow Up, I Want to Go to Boise*, Erma Bombeck records responses of a group of children with cancer and their brothers and sisters who were asked to imagine hope as an animal. "Hope has offsprings like any other animal," said one. "They're called 'Hopelets.' You don't keep them. You share them with other people who need one." Hope enters a hospital room with a pastoral minister—and hope doubles when there are two of you hoping.

Avoiding Bedpans and Breakfast

Consider the day's schedule as you plan your visit. Early mornings are busy times in health-care facilities. Baths, breakfast, linen changes and medications fill the day's first hours.

When you arrive, you might check with the nursing staff concerning the condition of the patient. "She had a rough night" or "He just learned the doctor is discharging him tomorrow" gives you hints about how the patient may be feeling.

As you approach the room, remember that a national poll revealed that hospital patients' number-one complaint is lack of privacy. If the door is closed, knock. Wait for a response before entering. If you know that the person is hard-of-hearing, open the door and identify yourself. Always ask if this is a good time for a short visit. Someone perched on a bedpan may not be ready for meaningful conversation.

Closed curtains around the bed usually indicate that some aspect of care is going on. If in doubt, knock on the open door. State your mission and ask if the timing is right. If the answer is no, ask if and when you may return.

Proper and adequate introductions are important: "Good morning, I'm Patti from St. Suburb Parish and a volunteer for the hospital chaplain." Your introduction should tell who you are, who sent you and, if necessary for your particular ministry, your Church affiliation. They provide you with both identity and authority. Proper identification is essential even when visiting your own parishioners. Pain, fatigue, medication or age may diminish a patient's ability to recognize you or to comprehend your mission. Be clearer in introducing yourself than I once was!

Mr. Ryan was engrossed in his newspaper when I knocked and entered the room, saying, "Hello, I'm Patti from Pastoral Care."

No response.

"I thought I'd stop by to see how things are going with you today."

No response. I had two strikes and didn't want to go down swinging. I waited. Perhaps he was finishing an engrossing article in the paper. Still no response. Over the top of the paper I glimpsed a pair of angry eyes. Maybe he was perturbed by my interruption.

"I'm sorry to interrupt you this morning, but before I leave I would like to offer you Communion."

"Communion! You mean you aren't from the insurance company?"

Shortly before my arrival at Mr. Ryan's room, his insurance company had informed him by phone that they would not cover his current hospitalization. In response to his great displeasure, the company had promised they would send an agent to the hospital to discuss his situation.

Enter one chaplain. Mr. Ryan's angry mood and my inadequate introduction ("Pastoral Care" meant "insurance company" to him at that moment) created the illusion that I was the "enemy" who had just denied him a sizable sum of money.

We shared a hearty, stress-reducing laugh over the case of mistaken identity. Mr. Ryan received Communion—and the insurance agent probably received a much more cordial welcome upon arrival.

How to address the patient is another question. Is "Mr. Smith" more appropriate than "John"? Using the surname is respectful; one usually uses the formal name with a person one doesn't know well. Yet "John" may be a friendlier approach.

You might begin by addressing the patient by surname. As conversation moves to a level of confidence, you might ask, "Do you mind if I call you John?" Or continue to call him Mr. Smith throughout the visit. When praying with him, it seems more appropriate to use his baptismal name, "John."

Follow your instincts. Each of us must determine the comfort level with baptismal or surnames. Your age, the age of the patient, your particular role as visitor will all affect your decision. What *feels* appropriate is probably the best choice.

Roommates

In rooms accommodating more than one patient, a greeting to a patient's roommate is appropriate. An inquiry about how the roommate is feeling is an opportunity to spread the Church's care to others. Inviting the roommate to join in prayer fosters a spirit of concern.

As I entered one double room, I found the curtain

pulled between the two beds. The occupants were in a heated conversation with each other. Accusations were flying around the room. "You people don't care about us!" "You don't know what it's like to be...." I felt as if I had entered a battlefield rather than a hospital room.

The patient I was assigned to visit began to talk with me. Soon we were discussing the heated exchange I had interrupted. From behind the curtain the other patient interjected his opinions. I found myself standing at the end of the curtain serving as interpreter between two angry men.

Finally I prepared to leave, feeling not much had been accomplished. I asked the two if they would like to join in prayer. Both readily agreed. We prayed for understanding of all people and for the ability to see each other as God sees us. In conclusion the "Our Father" echoed from both sides of the drawn curtain.

On my next visit the same situation presented itself, though the arguments had toned down. On subsequent visits I found the men talking to each other in friendly conversation. I suggested that it might be easier for them to talk if the curtain were pulled back. They agreed.

On my last visit with them, both were regretting that they would be discharged the next day. They had become friends who were sorry to part. They had exchanged phone numbers so that they could keep in touch when they reached home. During their hospital stays these men had learned to put aside racial and religious prejudices and to love each other.

Assessing the Mood

A quick assessment of the room will enable you to begin to determine the patient's mood. Are the shades pulled or does the sunlight shine in? A dark, closed room may indicate pain or a sense of isolation. Is the patient actively doing anything—reading, watching TV, talking on the phone? All may indicate interest in communicating with the outside world. What signs exist that others know and care that the person is in this place? Are there cards, drawings by children or grandchildren, flowers, personal items? All these indicators tell something about the individual's connectedness with the world beyond the hospital room. The environment may reveal what type of support system the patient has—and the level of support affects the patient's outlook and feelings about the present situation.

A soft cheerfulness is a safe tone for your entry. A too-cheerful approach may stir resentment: "Why is she so cheerful when I feel so rotten?" A too-dour attitude may depress the patient: "If he looks so glum, I must be sicker than I thought I was."

Commenting on the patient's appearance is not advisable. One who looks terrific to you may be feeling like last Thanksgiving's mashed potatoes. A comment about a positive appearance does little to establish enough rapport to discuss feelings. The patient will only think that you are out of tune.

As your conversation proceeds, your facial expressions will reflect whether you are truly hearing what the patient has to share with you. Mirror the patients' feelings, allowing them to see themselves more clearly: Smile at accounts of happy aspects; remain serious as they share difficulties. The *patient* is responsible for the tone of the visit. *You* are accountable for listening to that tone, reflecting it to the patient and responding to it.

What Shall We Talk About?

Assume that the patient is experiencing some level of stress at being hospitalized. Alteration of daily life patterns creates stress and anxiety, whether it is recognized by the patient or not. People cope with that stress according to their personality and their condition—with bright, cheerful optimism; grouchy complaining; quiet acceptance.

The initial visit is an occasion to explore the person's feelings about the current situation. Very simple statements or questions serve to begin the conversation. "I've stopped by to see how things are going for you today" may bring a torrent of comments about how confused the patient feels, about what tests and treatments are being conducted. Then you have a starting point for exploring the apparent feelings of frustration and confusion.

Another person may simply respond, "OK." Using your observations of the room atmosphere, the appearance of the patient and any information you have on the patient's condition, you will need to explore with the patient what OK means: "OK can be better than you felt yesterday or it can be not as good. Which does it mean for you?" Gentle verbal probing encourages the patient to tell you (and admit to herself) what is actually transpiring within her being.

On the other hand, the patient may tell you with great pride about the number of kidney stones the doctor removed yesterday, thankful that the source of pain is removed. Or joy may overflow because the suspected heart attack was actually an ailment of much less threatening origin.

Patients are free to tell you exactly what their feelings are because you have asked. Your caring questions can be release valves for stress, enabling hospitalization to result in emotional and spiritual growth for the patient. Above all, trust your own conversational style. Be yourself—as Josh was.

Josh visited all new patients admitted to the hospital. Walking from room to room was a labor of love, due to his own physical limitations. No one would ever have known how painful it was for him to make his rounds, judging from the smile on his face. As he delivered packets of information regarding pastoral care, he frequently asked patients, "How are you today?" Those who responded, "Fine," he would challenge with a twinkle in his eyes, "Then what are you doing in the hospital?" His simple humor, though often repeated, always brought a smile to the patient's face. From there the conversation flowed.

Establishing a Plan

We come as pastoral care visitors representing a parish, a particular faith or the hospital for which we volunteer.

As we listen, we may develop a sense of the spiritual basis of a person's life. The fact that an individual indicated a religious preference on the hospital admitting form does not necessarily indicate a strong spiritual connection with that religion. Likewise, a lack of religious identification may not signify an absence of faith. Because we cannot *assume* the level of religious connectedness, we must always rely on the patient to articulate it.

As you introduce yourself as a visitor from St. Loveisall Parish, a patient may set the scene by saying she hasn't been to church in thirty years. Your presence speaks the Church's concern for her welfare regardless of her longstanding absence. Provide the patient with the opportunity to express her reasons for leaving the worshiping community. Open expression is the first step in healing alienation from the Church.

Your plan and your ministry depend heavily upon your acceptance of the person just as he is. Ask yourself and ask God, "What does this person need at this time that I may be able to provide?"

One man claimed, "I don't need God! He's for people who can't *handle* their own problems."

The visitor agreed, "You are so right. God *is* for those who can't manage everything themselves—and I guess I'm one of those people."

Silence followed. Then the patient replied, "Come to think of it, I haven't done so well with my life either." A space was opened for an awareness of God to enter into the man's life.

Another patient just sobbed. Katie tried to stop, but the tears flowed continually. What could I say? Words seemed to intensify the tears. A phrase came to mind, "Create silence." That seemed to be the wisdom for the moment. She clutched my hand. The silence was punctuated by her sobs. Finally, they became fewer and farther between, then they ceased with a sigh. "Thank you," she said gratefully. "I just needed someone to let me cry." That time created trust between us and we later had many long visits when we talked about God's presence in her life.

Much later I ran across the words of philosopher Søren Kierkegaard that had popped into my mind:

> If I were a doctor and were asked for my advice, I should reply: Create silence! Bring people to silence, the word of God cannot be heard in the noisy world of today. And even if it were blazoned forth with all the panoply of noises so that it could be heard in the midst of all the other noise, then it would no longer be the Word of God. Therefore, create silence.

Someone recently asked if I knew that the words *silent* and *listen* contain the same letters—just rearranged. That scrap of trivia says something about the relationship between silence and listening. Silence creates the atmosphere in which thoughts, like the letters of those two words, can be rearranged. Listening even when no words are being spoken gives respect to a person's thoughts. This special kind of silence is not a dead silence in which nothing transpires. It is punctuated by your perceptive questions and comments: "You seem to be thinking some very deep thoughts." "What part of being hospitalized is the most difficult for you to understand or accept?"

Your questions are refined versions of the old offer, "A penny for your thoughts." Such queries and comments do not arise from curiosity, but from a desire to enable the patient to hear his own thoughts. These empower him to delve within himself for a better understanding of who he is at this moment in life. You want to enable him to tell *himself* where he is emotionally and spiritually. Then you can assure him that you have heard him. With the assurance that he is acceptable as he is, he is free to move beyond the present feelings and become a stronger individual. He can grasp strength from the fact that even though he is frightened, he still has the potential for courage; that though he is physically weak, he has untapped spiritual and emotional power to call upon.

Some patients will tell you exactly what they want and need. Wilma always asked, "Will you pray for me?" Never say yes unless you intend to follow through with that commitment.

Tony was very old and very poor. He had no family and most of his friends were dead or unable to visit him. His greatest comfort besides a vibrant faith was a little dog. Could someone please call his neighbor who had promised to care for Trixie to see how she was? Receiving Communion and knowing that Trixie was OK gave Tony courage to face another day with a severely deteriorating heart.

Hearing With Your Heart

Don't try to help too much. The wisest course is to do for others only what they cannot do themselves—and nothing more. Doing for others what they are capable of doing themselves fosters a dependency that destroys confidence. Such pampering debilitates an individual until the person feels weak and incapable.

From an anonymous author comes a piece of wisdom called "Listen":

> When I ask you to listen to me
>   and you start giving me advice,
>   you have not done what I asked.
> When I ask you to listen to me
>   and you begin to tell me why I shouldn't feel that way,
>   you are trampling on my feelings.
> When I ask you to listen to me
>   and you feel you have to do something to solve
>   my problems,
>   you have failed me, strange as that may seem.
> Listen! All I asked was that you listen,
>   not to talk or do—just hear me.
> Advice is cheap: 10 cents will get you both
>   Dear Abby and Billy Graham in the same newspaper.
> And I can do for myself; I'm not helpless.
> Maybe discouraged and faltering,
>   but not helpless.
> But when you accept as a simple fact
>   that I do feel what I feel,
>   no matter how irrational,
>   then I quit trying to convince you
>   and get about the business of understanding
>   what's behind this irrational feeling.
> And when that's clear, the answers are obvious

and I don't need advice.
Irrational feelings make sense when we understand
  what's behind them.
Perhaps that's why prayer works, sometimes,
    for some people
      because God is mute,
      and he doesn't give advice
      or try to fix things.
  He just listens and lets you work it out for yourself.
So, please listen and just hear me, and,
    if you want to talk, wait a minute for your turn:
    and I'll listen to you.

Sirach expressed your purpose well when he wrote,
"Happy is he who finds a friend, and he who speaks to
attentive ears" (Sirach 25:9). You come as a *friend* to the
sick on your visits—if your ears are well tuned. Many
people worry about what they will *say* to others; few are
as concerned about how they will *hear* others. As you
explore with the patient the feelings that surround the
circumstances of hospitalization, listen actively with
your ears and hear with your eyes and heart as well.
Active listening is heart listening—caring about the
deepest concerns of the patient's heart and treasuring
those concerns with confidence in your own heart.

Reading Body Language

Active listening indicates that you are involved in what
the patient is saying. Your body posture is oriented
toward the person so that you can see the patient and the
patient can view you with minimal effort. Many

messages are transmitted by eye contact. The words you hear enter through your ears *and* eyes because the patient's body language will convey as much as the verbal language does.

Is she clutching the sheet as she tells you everything is OK? Her hands indicate something is not OK. You can respond, "Your words tell me you are OK, but your hands seem a bit anxious." Be willing to wait for a response.

The mouth may be smiling, but you see tears welling up in his eyes. "I'm getting a mixed message. I see a smiling mouth and tears waiting to spill. Would you like to talk about that?" Maybe yes and maybe no. Whatever the response, the patient has the comfort of knowing that you have noticed an underlying feeling and that you care.

An untouched lunch tray bears a message. Ask about it. One man replied, "I miss my wife's cooking so much since she's gone. Nothing tastes good to me." A whole area of conversation opened regarding the loss that this man has faced since his wife's death.

One who looks at the floor or away from the speaker in a distant manner may be experiencing depression. Keep in mind that medications can also affect patients' alertness.

Recognizing Internal Processing

Regardless of your skill as a pastoral care visitor, you will encounter patients who do not choose to talk about their situations. You may have an urge to keep trying to encourage the patient to open up. But such perseverance may be an intrusion into the patient's privacy. Some people process life's events and their meanings within themselves quite well. Their reluctance to share with others does not indicate denial of what is happening in their lives or emotions that are stuffed within themselves. They may be individuals who ponder what transpires at great length before they talk about them—if, indeed, they ever choose to discuss them. One such woman told me, "I don't know what I know until I have time alone to think it through."

Encountering such patients does not discredit your visiting skills. Accept the fact that the patient who is reluctant to talk about deep issues may have a preferred confidante or may possess a powerful internal forum in which to process the meaning of life. Respect for the internal processor is essential. The best you can do may be to offer a thought or a question for such a person to consider privately without feeling obliged to respond verbally.

Communicating Understanding

Active listening means responding to what you hear. Your response assures the patient that you are *with* him or her at this moment. As the patient communicates her feelings about her predicament, communicate your understanding of what you believe you have heard:

> *Patient:* Nobody knows what is going on around here! One person tells me this and another says

something else. It's ridiculous!

Visitor: It sounds like you feel really left out of the plans for your treatment.

Patient: You bet I do! And it really makes me angry.

Finally someone has heard the patient's complaints about feeling isolated and helpless concerning treatment. Having an ally is a comfort. You may not be able to remedy the communication gap that exists between patient and caregivers, yet you have offered an opportunity to vent feelings about the circumstances without being judged for attitude. Some stress has been relieved.

Many conversations are stunted when participants mentally formulate their responses to what the other person is saying before they have actually listened to the message. The listening energy and focus that the speaker deserves is misdirected to the mind of the listener who busily plots the next wise response. The result of this style of conversation is that as one speaks, the other hears with the mouth rather than the ears, and little is communicated. The human mind is a wondrous thing to run around in—but not when your mission is to absorb and understand the message of another.

Accurate listening solves many problems. One eucharistic minister entered a room in the maternity unit to find a new mother sobbing while her husband attempted to comfort her. The husband quickly told the visitor why his wife and he were so upset.

"Little Andrew was born last night and things just aren't right. He's so little and helpless. They tell us he's going to be very retarded."

"I can understand why you are both so upset. Your hopes for your baby have been changed dramatically," the visitor responded.

"We're sad that he is this way, but he's *ours* and we'll love him no matter what! But now they tell us that we won't be able to keep him. We have to put him in some kind of a home for babies like him."

This idea did not sound accurate to the visitor. She explained to the couple that she would like to check on this information for them. Going to the nurses' station, she explained what she had been told.

"Oh, no," the charge nurse explained. "We thought they were upset about the extra care this baby will require of them. We explained that if they could not care for him, there might be a place for him in an infants' home for babies with special needs like his."

The nurse and the visitor returned to the mother's room. The nurse unraveled the misunderstanding about little Andrew's destination after he was released from the nursery. Indeed, he could go home with them, she reassured the parents. And a courageous young couple began plans to care for a child whom they would love no matter what his limitations and special needs.

When the couple had a second child two years later, the same hospital volunteer encountered them again. The hope they had expressed in the first hours of Andrew's life had not diminished. They rejoiced in each bit of Andrew's progress as they shared his story with the volunteer. The new baby would be one more person in the family to love Andrew and be loved by him.

Affirming Strengths

Attentive and active listening invites the patient to speak in a manner that will enable better self-knowledge. You can affirm the strengths that you see in people who may consider themselves weak.

One minister's view of a woman's abilities helped build her capacity to cope and to recognize herself not as weak and hopeless but as having attributes that serve her during hospitalization.

Marie almost whispered to her parish visitor, "Do you know what I did this morning?"

The visitor replied, "No. What did you do?"

The elderly woman answered, "I said I would *not* have my bath before I ate breakfast."

The declaration seemed unimportant. Yet the visitor sensed this statement represented a breakthrough for Marie. She responded, "That sounds like a declaration of independence to me, Marie."

Marie smiled and softly said, "For me it is. I've never been able to decide anything for myself. First my mother and father, then my husband...." Marie went on to describe a life dominated by others who made choices for her. This hospitalization was virtually her first time alone. She was using it positively to make decisions for herself. Marie would leave the hospital a stronger, more confident woman.

Evoking Feelings

Invite patients to speak of their concerns about illness and its ramifications in their lives. Patients may be reluctant to discuss these concerns openly with family or friends because they want to protect them from sadness or difficult information. "I'm fine" or "Everything is going great!" may be smokescreen responses. Some of the most smiling, apparently confident patients may be a breath away from tears of fear. Others suppress with iron-willed determination any display of fear. But what is suppressed by the human mind will escape by another route—as physical symptoms or psychological disturbances.

In Mark's account of Jesus casting out the demon from the Gerasene man who lived among the tombs (Mark 5:1-20), Jesus asks the demon its name. Commenting on the story in *Transforming Body and Soul: Therapeutic Wisdom in the Gospel Healing Stories*, priest-psychotherapist Steven Galipeau explores the value of naming what troubles us.

> We notice in this healing story and in others involving a demon that Jesus talks to it. Here he asks, "What is your name?" From a psychological perspective this is a crucial question. Naming something makes it *real*.
>
> The more conscious we are of the dynamics inside us, the more we can cast aside "unclean spirits" so that the Spirit of God can flow through us. The less conscious we are of such things, the more they rule our lives, and the less centered in God we are likely to be.

Inviting patients to name their fears of pain, of loss of income, of dependence on others or of death gives them power over the demons they name. Demons of fear and doubt thrive in the dark of denial. Brought to the light of conscious recognition and shared with another person, they diminish. Further, fear almost always fosters anger. Allowing the underlying causes of fear to surface also calms anger. Probing questions and statements which enable patients to bring their demons of concern from the dark of denial to the dawn of conscious awareness affirm that you hear their message with understanding.

"Jeremy, how do you feel about the doctor's diagnosis?" the visitor inquired.

"I think I'll be able to handle it," Jeremy responded with his usually booming voice.

"It's good to know you think you can handle it. How do you *feel* about the situation?"

After a pause, Jeremy said—more quietly this time, "It scares the hell out of me!"

The patient had retreated into the safe haven of the mind in telling the pastoral visitor what he *thought* about his diagnosis. The visitor wisely assured him that she had heard what he said. She then returned to the question about *feelings*.

While it may not by scientifically accurate to say it, feelings seem to originate in the gut. Unless digested, they lodge there, creating spiritual and psychological indigestion. Yet we often hesitate to free them. A temptation common to visitors as well as patients is to begin searching mentally for a solution. But one of the blessings of pastoral care is that its primary purpose is not to "fix" people's problems. We are incapable of accomplishing that feat. We are to support them in the feelings that rise within them. Feelings are neither right nor wrong. They simply *are.*

Feelings vital to the patient may be taking second place to what is going on physiologically. Providing spiritual support gives others the strength to search for their own solutions to a problem. An individual who resolves his or her own dilemma gains strength and self-esteem through taking charge of life. As a pastoral care visitor, consider this valuable support as "spiritual splinting." We help bear the burden through our presence and understanding, through prayer and compassion, so that the other person does not break under the weight of a concern.

If each snowflake that falls has its own unique configuration, it is not less surprising to realize that each person has a unique response to life's joys and sorrows, reliefs and stresses. Because of the infinite uniqueness of humans, we can never hope to know exactly how another feels in a given situation. You may have suffered the loss of an unborn child at exactly the same trimester as the woman you visit; she may be precisely the same age you were. But even with multiple similarities, the impact of the loss will be different for the two of you. We can *never* say in truth, "I know how you feel." We can only know how *we* feel.

Your own life experiences still have valid meaning in our attempts to support others, however. Loss as well as joy formed you into a caring, compassionate visitor who comes to share the moment with another. Times may arise when it is appropriate to share a *short* chapter of your own story. Just think carefully before you share: Do not divert attention from the patient's feelings to your own. If you speak of your own miscarriage, the woman may be reluctant to talk about her loss for fear of renewing your pain. Yet, if it seems appropriate, knowledge that you have walked through a similar painful time may enable the bereft mother to speak her sadness.

If you do not understand what the patient is trying to say, be honest. Say so. That is more helpful than putting words into the patient's mouth as you grope for their meaning. In this way you also reaffirm your desire to understand the patient. At the same time, the patient is requested to restate the feelings. Ambiguity may be present in the mind of the patient as well as your own. Gently probing without intruding can encourage a patient to share a bit more deeply or to define feelings more explicitly.

> *Patient:* In a way I'm glad to be in the hospital. Maybe they'll appreciate me more. You know how that is.
>
> *Visitor:* I don't know how that is for you. Would you like to tell me?
>
> *Patient:* Well, our marriage hasn't been what you'd call great for a long time....

Too many questions can give the patient a feeling of being grilled and drilled. Empathetic statements—"It sounds lonely at your house"; "Not knowing what is wrong with you can be frightening"—coupled with an occasional question keep the conversation flowing.

Allow time for the patient to sift through the feelings

that surface before answering. A sense of hurry stifles opening up emotions. The psalmist advises simply, "Be still, and know that I am God!" (Psalm 46:10a, *New Revised Standard Version Bible*). Give God time to speak in the quiet of patients' hearts as they come in touch with their feelings.

Respect the patients. Your goal is not to press them to share confidences they are not ready to talk about. Respect also means being nonjudgmental. Cultivate the ability to be genuinely caring no matter what the life-style or values of the patient may be. Your task is to enable people to come in touch with their personhood— who they are at this particular moment of life.

After naming the demon, the gut-level feeling, the patient will probably seem relieved. Relief may be expressed through tears or visible relaxing of body tension. Hands release the corner of the sheet; shoulders settle. The patient may admit to former resistance to acknowledging the feeling: "I didn't realize how that has been stored up in me!" or "I never thought I'd tell anyone that." The feelings themselves will not evaporate. They will wash over patients as they struggle with new awareness of themselves. This is a much healthier tension than the stress of unnamed feelings that gnaw at one's sense of security and well-being.

Naming feelings and exposing them to the light of consciousness opens an emotional and spiritual space within patients. They are then able to recognize their own power over emotions by naming and discussing them. Fear or concern has not triumphed. A place for faith exists.

Speaking of Faith

A 93-year-old woman knew she was near death. She was tired and ready to go. Only one problem remained: her son. He could not accept her approaching death and begged her not to give up, even though she told him repeatedly that she was tired and would welcome death's freedom. He could not say good-bye and set her free. She remarked, "He acts like there isn't a resurrection!" Time is but a piece of life. The son could only see his mother's life in time, not in eternity.

Though the woman's son was a regular churchgoer, his faith at the approach of death varied from his mother's. Faith wears many faces. We have faith that the elevator we enter will carry us promptly to the floor we select. We have faith that the airliner we board will bear us safely to our destination. We have faith that the sun will rise tomorrow and the moon will go through a given sequence during the month. Our faith that these events will occur is founded on the experience that past happenings will be repeated.

When we witness a wedding, we have faith that a marriage of permanence will result. Yet when we recall the many divorces that mar the permanence of marriage, our faith quakes a bit. We have faith our car will start when we switch the ignition—unless it is a twelve-year-old model with 178,000 miles on it that never starts readily and sometimes does not start at all. Once again experience shapes faith.

Faith in the face of illness is confronted with similar challenges. People believe they will always be healthy if wellness has been their basic life pattern. They may believe that good health is God's gift. When illness or an accident robs them of that gift which they believe is from God, their faith quakes.

Fear and faith are in some ways antonyms. As opposites, they cannot *totally* coexist in a person. But people need not feel guilty because fear grips their lives during difficult days. Faith is not perfected in us. We have said that naming the fear that impinges on faith diminishes the power that fear holds. When fear is recognized, a spiritual space opens for the growth of a more mature faith tailored to the stage of life through which the patient is passing. The renewed faith is based not only on what has been in the past, but also on what is at the present and what can be in the future.

Pastoral visitors have a unique opportunity to walk with patients as they discover a more mature faith growing where their former faith languished. A temptation may arise to inject patients with a dose of your own faith to enable them more quickly to arrive at a new faith in God. The liability of this approach is that all you can provide is *your* faith, not someone else's. Such an injection may cause a negative reaction, a rejection of faith. Your goal is to move to how the patient *feels* about her condition. Together you discover and build upon her faith in order to support and strengthen her.

Flying with our three-year old son Dan provided a brief lesson in theology for us. Feeling the excitement of the moment and the thrust of the aircraft as we soared skyward, Dan warned in a very loud voice, "Look out, God! Here we come and we don't want to run over ya!"

When things are going well in life, we may feel a bit that way ourselves. We feel the power and exhilaration of success and prosperity. But when illness or injury stops the forward motion of life's journey, we may be more inclined to fear that God may be "running over" us. We need a healthy image of God and of God's relationship to us if we are to avoid that run-over feeling. Unveiling the patient's image of God is part of good pastoral care. Only when we have established a rapport with the patient and have a basis of trust do we dare enter the hallowed ground of personal beliefs.

Some gently probing questions may begin the exploration of the relationship with God. Asking "Where is God in all of this for you?" may elicit a variety of responses: "Nowhere!" "He put me here because I deserve this." "Right with me—keeps me going one day at a time." "He sends all these great people to care for me and my family."

Any response, no matter how negative or positive, indicates a starting point. Each represents the seed of faith which is to be nurtured for growth. Each answer reveals an aspect of faith. Each individual is saying in some manner, "I do believe; help my unbelief!" (Mark 9:24b). Even the most dogged doubter is stating belief by complaining that God is unavailable in the present situation. Through gently probing conversation, attempt to enlighten his unbelief.

Many patients are not ready to speak of God. Life's hurts, rejections, failures have dimmed their concept of God. God-talk may only solidify their denial of God's presence in their lives. In such cases—as indeed in all pastoral care visits—we are called to be Christ to the patient.

To be Christ is to come as a loving, accepting

embodiment of the Spirit of God. To be Christ is to accept the patient and his or her potential for holiness. To be Christ is to be a healing person who, through listening, absorbs, responds to and forgives the person's shared story. Introducing yourself as a representative of your Christian faith affords the opportunity to represent the Christian community to the patient. Without *preaching* the gospel you can *become* the Good News through your pastoral care visits. Each pastoral care visit is a trialogue, a three-way conversation in which three voices resound even when only two seem to be present.

Why Me?

Sooner or later a patient will look you straight in the eye and defiantly demand, "Why me?" Or twisting the corner of a blanket, look wistfully out the window and murmur in a soft, pleading tone, "Why me?" Relax. "Why me?" is a question you do not have to answer. You cannot. No answer exists. Yet posing this question is a valuable step to the individual seeking an understanding of an illness.

Poet Rainer Maria Rilke once suggested that, when questions tear at our hearts, we should try to love the questions themselves. Loving the question "Why me?" means exploring it, turning it this way and that in thought. This enables the question to become an avenue to God.

"Why me?" may underlie the strong self-image of one who has tried to live an involved life in a spirit of mercy and kindness according to God's direction as she understands it. In spite of her best efforts she has encountered a tough obstacle in life's journey. "Why me?" may also spring from the thoughts of one who has already known much suffering and wonders quietly why he must face more anguish.

Allow the patient's question to rebound. "Why do *you* believe this has happened to you?" After careful thought one patient responded, "Why not me? I've lived a pretty rotten life—kicked God around a lot." Such an honest confession of a life-style not focused on God is an initial step in reconciliation. The opportunity awaits for the patient to meet a God of mercy and forgiveness, a God who loves the patient regardless of past offenses. Such a person may be open at this time to learn of a God who "so loved the world that he gave his only Son" (John 3:16a) to bridge the chasm of sin with salvation.

If the patient's experience is of a distant, uncaring or totally absent God, your caring, accepting presence may be the most positive word you can speak at this particular time. God-talk may drive the patient who does not feel loved and accepted deeper into despair.

The patient who reflects on the question "Why me?" may discover neglect of care for the body and begin to recognize that abusing alcohol or drugs, smoking, overeating or underexercising have contributed to the illness. A very *un*official survey I conducted over a period of several months revealed that at least two-thirds of the patients I visited were hospitalized at least in some part due to some form of self-neglect. A diabetic confessed eating and drinking what he wanted rather than what his body could tolerate ("Nobody's going to tell me what I can eat!"). Some heart patients suffer from angry hearts that will not forgive past hurts and their perpetrators. The stress of unforgiveness seems to clog the lifelines of their bodies. Lung cancer patients and emphysema sufferers smoked while denying the validity of research linking their habits to disease. Individuals with circulatory problems refuse dietary and exercise routines because "it probably won't help anyway."

Those patients who do begin to discern self-neglect will need to forgive themselves for not loving themselves more. Self-care becomes possible for those who see themselves as worthy of good care. Hope is what we can offer them—hope that they are worthy of good health, hope that they do indeed have some control over their attitudes toward the body and its care.

Seeking to understand suffering is the essential meaning of the "Why me?" question. Hospital chaplain Cornelius G. Remple developed nine maxims which define his view of suffering. The essence of them follows:

1) Suffering is not God's desire for us, but occurs in the process of life.

2) Suffering is not given to teach us something, but we do learn through it.

3) Suffering is not given to us to teach others something, but they, too, may learn through it.

4) Suffering is not given to punish us, but it is sometimes the consequence of poor judgment or sin.

5) Suffering does not occur because our faith is weak, but through it our faith may be strengthened.

6) Suffering is not God's way to achieve the divine

purposes, but through suffering God's purposes are sometimes achieved.

7) Suffering is not always to be avoided at all costs, but it is sometimes chosen.

8) Suffering can either destroy us or add meaning to life.

9) The will of God has more to do with how we respond to life than with how life deals with us.

Helplessness and hopelessness of physical recovery were apparent in the life of my friend, Dick. Life ebbed in this formerly vital, active, fun-loving man, who in his final years was able to do nothing for himself—except smile. Yet through years of struggle with his disease he never asked, "Why me?" He fought the disease with medical treatment, exercise, diet and a remarkably optimistic outlook while realistically accepting his fate. As his physical abilities failed, his faith flourished. His life and the lives of those who knew him were sculpted by his suffering. While my fear was of losing my friend, another underlying fear lurked. If this could happen to him, it could happen to me. Self-preservation is powerful. I never heard him ask, "Why me?" But I asked again and again, "Why him?" You too will probably find yourself asking, "Why?" Love the question. Ponder it.

When the patient has had the opportunity to explore "Why me?" to his or her satisfaction, you can offer a new question: What? "What can you do for yourself to make today more manageable?" "What do you need that someone else can assist you with?"

Or ask *how*: "How can you learn to eat, dress, care for yourself with your right hand only?" Or *who*: "Who

needs you?" "Who can you rely on for support?" Or
when: "When you faced other difficulties in life, how did
you overcome them?" Properly used the *how, who, when*
and *what* questions build a foundation of hope and
support for the future. They enable patients to tap the
resources of strength, energy, faith, ability and
knowledge that remain in reserve within them.

Assessing Spiritual Needs

Eileen's body wore the marks of congestive heart failure,
inoperable cancer and rheumatoid arthritis. Yes, she
said, she would very much like to pray with me. Keenly
aware of the extent of her needs, I asked if she had
anything in particular she would like to bring to God in
prayer. Without hesitation she smiled triumphantly and
replied, "Oh, yes! I'd like to thank God for the health that
is within me!"

This wise and faithful woman's positive view of her
life focused on what was good. A remnant of good health
gave her life and energy for that moment. She could look
beyond a body plagued by multiple debilitating and
life-threatening illnesses to celebrate the health that
remained in her frail body. As we prayed together, we
also thanked God for the health of her spirit. None of her
physical ailments had stricken that spirit.

Eileen shows us how easily we can err in assessing
spiritual needs. An easy assumption would have been to
imagine that Eileen wanted to *ask* God for something.
But her spiritual need was to praise God. Eileen's life
reflects Paul's admonition, "Rejoice always. Pray without

ceasing. In all circumstances give thanks, for this is the will of God for you in Christ Jesus" (1 Thessalonians 5:16-18).

We must be careful not to impose upon patients what we believe they need. Above all, we cannot force God or "God-talk" upon them. Knowing that you represent a community of faith may open the conversation for the patient: "Well, you know I haven't been to church for thirty years." "My faith is all I have going for me right now." "God's giving me what I deserve." Each statement reveals the faith stance of the speaker. You have the opportunity to lead an exploration of views of God. Seeing another rediscover or reaffirm that God is a God of love who forgives and invites us to return is a graced moment in ministry.

The Place of Prayer

Prayer is central to the pastoral care visit. Prayer sends us forth on our mission to the sick. Whether offered aloud while we are with the patient or silently after we leave, it is at the heart of healing. Prayer enables us to release each patient and his needs to God when the visit is completed. Each pastoral care visit is in its own way a prayer—a communion of God with his people. In spite of the essential nature of prayer it is wise to pray concisely and particularly for the patient when we are with him or her. Lengthy prayers may lift your spirits to the very threshold of heaven. They may only succeed in exhausting a sick person.

Prayer may be as integral to our personal lives as

breathing. But when we enter a patient's room, prayer is an offering made only with the patient's consent.

One young woman expressed great anger at a pastoral care visitor who entered her room uninvited while she was being tended by medical staff. She was embarrassed to have another person in the room during the examination. She became further incensed when the visitor began to pray aloud for her. The visitor intended only good. The result did not match that intent. The woman requested that no pastoral care visitors be admitted to her room in the future.

The damage in this case arose from the visitor placing her need to pray for the patient ahead of the patient's need for prayer at that time. Sensitivity to patients' needs is the foremost responsibility no matter how much you believe a patient needs prayer. Do not impose prayer on a patient.

At the conclusion of your visit ask, "Could I offer a prayer for you?" One woman responded to that question, "Honey, *I'll* pray and *you* listen!" And pray she did. I realized I was in the presence of one whose life was an ongoing communication with God. We shared a hallowed moment. If the response to the question about prayer is yes, ask further, "Is there anything you would especially like to pray for?"

The prayer you offer for and with the patient will reflect your own personal prayer style. Some of us pray in a conversational style, talking to an ever-present God. We offer thanks for the good that has happened. We ask God to hear the patient's needs. We may allow a space of silence for the patient's prayer and conclude with a familiar prayer, such as The Lord's Prayer.

Others feel more comfortable with traditional prayers of the Church that they know by heart or read from a book of prayers. Whenever possible, allow the patient to join in the prayers in voice as well as heart and mind.

What will you pray for—that the person be cured of all infirmity that very day? Such prayer sounds full of faith and power. Yet the patient's trust in the spiritual may be damaged if a cure does not follow prayer requests. And we know that not everyone for whom we pray recovers physically.

The essential task of pastoral care visits is to increase patients' awareness of God's presence in their lives. This is also the focus of prayer with patients. Prayer invites and recognizes God's presence. Prayer seeks forgiveness and reconciliation. Prayer searches for understanding. Prayer pleads for courage to endure pain. Prayer asks for peace. Above all prayer praises God.

In praying with the sick I have found that praising God in *all* things—not just in the good that comes our way but also through the difficult and the painful—has great merit. Some explanation of this prayer to the patient is helpful. In Philippians 4:4a, 6b St. Paul urges: "Rejoice in the Lord always...in everything, by prayer and petition, with thanksgiving, make your requests known to God." You do not want to create the misconception that we praise God *because* the patient is sick. Rather we praise God *in* the present circumstances and *through* the trials we face. This kind of prayer has power to keep us from being devastated by adversity. If we can still praise God when we are in pain and fear, we have triumphed spiritually over those evils in our lives. I cannot explain *why* this prayer is effective. It simply is.

If you do not know how to pray for a particular patient, be honest and say so. "Lord, there are times we do not know how to pray. We ask your Spirit to pray within us and for us...." Do not be afraid of silence in prayer. Acknowledge the silence and ask God to fill it in each of you.

Agnes was old, lonely and very poor. She had worked for years to pay debts left by an alcoholic husband; her only family was one niece. Then her eyesight dimmed and she had cataract surgery.

Agnes thought the pain she experienced in the days following surgery was the price of getting better. After all, she had experienced pain much of her life. She missed her follow-up check with the doctor because she didn't want to bother anyone to take her to the eye clinic. She figured that she would be able to take the bus the next week.

By the next week, however, the infection causing the pain had advanced to a crisis state. I visited her on the eve of the removal of her eye.

Agnes was terrified and angry. She thrashed in her bed and lashed out at everyone verbally—the parents who had abandoned her, the husband who had abused her, the niece who did not visit often enough. Then her anger turned to sadness and tears splashed her cheeks. She told me how useless she would always be—what could she do with only one eye?

I felt totally inept and helpless. I realized I could not repair Agnes' tattered life, but I wanted to leave her with a glimmer of hope, a shred of courage to take into surgery. We prayed together. I had no more words. Neither did Agnes.

I was leaving the room when another patient came to mind: Susan, a young mother newly diagnosed with multiple sclerosis. Susan had asked, "Please pray for me—and ask others to pray for me too." I saw risk in what I was considering: Asking Agnes to pray for Susan—asking her to do for someone else when she was so needy herself—might increase her anger. Yet the thought persisted. I felt compelled to ask.

"Agnes, there is someone in this hospital who needs you." She looked at me intently. I explained the situation without identifying Susan or violating any confidences.

"Why, I can do that!" Agnes' whole presence changed. The tension slipped from her face, leaving a peaceful smile. Gone was the anger. "Yes, I can do that all night until I fall asleep."

Agnes had found worth again. She had something important to do: A young mother needed her prayers. Agnes would still need to grieve the loss of her eye, but now she had hope.

I have used this request to help another by the gift of prayer many times. Every patient I have asked to pray for another has responded eagerly, with a kind of awe at the task asked of them. I choose patients for intercessory prayer for a number of reasons: Some, like Agnes, are so immersed in their own despair that praying for others seems to reach beyond their own pain. Others speak of what their prayer life means to them. Still others seem very sensitive to other people's needs. You will develop your own criteria if you decide to link people in this fashion.

Confidentiality is paramount. Patients from other units of the hospital are less identifiable. An initial rather than a name provides greater anonymity (God knows the individual's identity).

We are told that prayer does not change God. Prayer changes us. Developing prayer-patients is a way you can encourage the transforming power of prayer in others.

Special Needs of the Very Ill

"I think it will be days of rainbows and wishes and we will dance again with bright ribbons streaming and we will sing her favorite songs." Mary's young voice almost sang as she described the heaven where she believed her younger sister would soon be. The 13-year-old said she had thought a lot about heaven but that no one had ever asked her to tell them about it before. The opportunity to articulate her joyful thought gave Mary peace even in the midst of her sadness, hope to sustain her when Carla died.

Often the very sick have no opportunity to discuss the possibility of death. Loved ones "protect" them or fear being overwhelmed by their own emotions should the topic come up. The effort to comfort—"Now let's not talk that way. You're going to be just fine!"—actually robs the patient of the right to unburden herself of her fear of the future.

Ideally, initiating talk of approaching death lies with the patient. He may be reluctant to broach the subject. "Embarrassed," is how one patient described his feelings about talking about the possibility of death. "It's kind of like sitting here without any clothes on—a naked feeling." Death certainly is the ultimate nakedness, the final vulnerability. Yet its approach may seem less terrifying if one has named the fear and shared it with another person.

You may visit comatose patients who appear totally unaware of your presence. You may feel foolish at first, but a few words and perhaps a prayer of comfort may penetrate the unconscious state. If others are present, assume that the patient can hear all of your conversation concerning his condition. Much is still to be learned about the awareness level of the unconscious person, as the following story illustrates.

A woman made many hospital visits to an ailing relative. During her visits she noticed a patient in a room on the same corridor who was comatose. She began stopping on her visits to pray by the man's bedside. This continued for several weeks. One day as she passed the man's room, a voice called for her to come into the room. She was startled to realize it was the man for whom she had prayed. She entered the room and he said, "You're the lady who has come to pray for me so many times. Thank you so much." Her presence and prayers had reached him.

The Eucharist: Food for the Journey

If you come as a eucharistic minister, wait until the end of the visit to offer Communion. When you have talked a bit with the patient, the two of you will have created the smallest unit of Church: two called together in Christ's name. An even deeper sense of Church and community may be established if family members and friends who share the same faith are present and also wish to receive Communion. If the patient chooses to receive, offer Holy Communion and prayer, say your good-byes and quietly exit. Leave the patient with the Lord in an atmosphere of prayer and meditation.

See pages 127-131 for suggested Communion prayers.

Reconciliation

Having time for introspective thought coupled with facing their mortality often brings patients to realize their need for forgiveness. Even illness that is not life-threatening may awaken a patient to the need. Conversation may become confession as the patient delves into past memories.

You will hear confessions whether or not you are ordained. Edward Sellner, author of *Mentoring*, declares that his bartender father heard more confessions than the parish priest. You will join that trusted group which includes ordained ministers and priests, bartenders, beauticians, lovers and mothers. When you are privileged to share another's failings or sins, you are afforded a sacred moment in which to assure patients that God has always loved them and rejoices in their longing for forgiveness.

If the patient wishes sacramental reconciliation, contact the chaplain of the care facility to coordinate contact with the clergy.

Patients may seek your sanction to receive Holy Communion if they are uncertain of their status with their Church and with their God. This decision rests between the patient and God. No one else knows the condition of the patient's heart and soul. Suggest that the patient wait and pray about whether to receive the Eucharist if uncertainty exists. The ultimate responsibility is the patient's.

Anointing of the Sick

After being anointed and receiving Communion, Dorothy commented, "I feel so relieved—like I've got some extra strength to get well with. But if the Lord comes for me, I'm ready for him now."

Her words reflect a long journey toward understanding. When a parish visitor had first asked Dorothy whether she would like to be anointed, Dorothy responded angrily: "No! I'm not ready for that yet!" In her mid-seventies, her understanding of Anointing dated to her early upbringing. The very mention of the sacrament made her think, "Last rites! I must be on death's doorstep."

You may need to offer a good explanation to someone like Dorothy. The Anointing of the Sick is just that—for the *sick*, not just for the dying. Anointing is encouraged for anyone who because of advanced age or serious illness may benefit from it spiritually, physically or mentally.

Human beings are composed of body, mind and spirit. We are not fragments—a body separated from a mind apart from our spiritual selves. Because of this unity, when our bodies ache, our spirits and minds can also be affected. Conversely, when our spirits are touched with healing, our minds may release built-up stress and tension and our bodies begin to heal.

Anointing, while essentially a spiritual act, also has both physical and mental aspects. We are rubbed with oil, an ancient healing substance. We are offered words of Scripture and prayer that comfort our minds. The sacrament is intended to bring healing to the whole person: to put a mind at peace (mental healing); to renew energy and give the body strength (physical healing); and, if one should die, to make ready to meet the Lord (spiritual healing).

We are important parts of the Body of Christ. But illness or injury or age may separate us physically from that Body. The Sacrament of Anointing unites us with the entire worshiping Body, Christ's Church. If members of family or close friends can be present for the anointing, the reality of Church is even more apparent.

The Art of Departing

Knowing how and when to leave is an art. In the hospital visit you want to offer as much of your presence, your listening and your compassion as the patient requires without overstaying your welcome. Remember that you are the guest; the patient is the host. And the host may be tired or weak, in pain or discomfort, affected by medications. Lengthy visits can be exhausting. Your sensitivity to all of those qualifying factors determines the length of a visit. A very lonely person with few potential visitors may welcome a longer visit. One who has family and friends arriving in groups may cherish a few moments of quiet. Your observations will tell you when to depart.

Some patients seek to possess your time. Their symptoms are non-stop talking and often complaints about everything. You need to be able to recognize the manipulative, controlling patient. You do not help such individuals by allowing them to ramble on for excessive periods of time. You need to set boundaries for yourself and for the patients, firmly yet gently.

Joe had spent much of the pastor's visit raging at all the people who did not meet his expectations. The pastor had reflected with him on the pain, alienation and hopelessness Joe felt. Yet the patient was not ready to examine his role in fractured relationships or to forgive others.

With someone like Joe, you might depart this way: "I can see that you have been hurt by many people in your family. You know that we cannot change other people; we can only change ourselves. I hope your time in the hospital will give you the opportunity to learn how you can change to prevent their behavior from hurting you so much. I have someone else to see now. Would you like for us to pray about this situation before I leave?"

Humor in the Hospital

Humor is healing. Research indicates that laughter releases certain chemicals that aid the healing process.

Norman Cousins told the world about this phenomenon in *Anatomy of an Illness.*

Allow yourself the pleasure of laughing with patients where and when it is appropriate. Good taste is essential, of course. People who can laugh at themselves possess a healthy humility that may aid a healthy body. We, of course, can only laugh *with* them.

Mr. Winslow had been hospitalized for several weeks. The pastoral care volunteer had established a good rapport with him during their visits. As she prepared to see him one day, she could hear his doctor in the room. In fact, she could hear them as she came down the corridor. The doctor was emphatically telling Mr. Winslow that it was necessary for him to change his life-style if he wanted to live. Mr. Winslow was yelling his objections to the prescribed changes. "I'd rather be dead than do that!" he repeatedly hollered. The doctor assured him that he would be if he did not change his ways. As the doctor left, a parting "I'd rather be dead!" echoed down the hall.

Knowing the patient had a keen sense of humor, the volunteer followed a hunch as she entered the room. "I'm here again from the chaplain's office. It sounds like I'm just in time to help you plan your funeral." Her hunch paid off. The patient looked surprised, then began to laugh. They spent their time discussing how difficult the changes in diet, exercise, work habits and attitude were going to be for Mr. Winslow. Laughing and sharing the frustration reduced his resistance to the new plan for his life.

Hospitals harbor humor if we allow it to flow. The human story is enlivened by humor that keeps us from taking ourselves and our problems too seriously. Humor properly applied reduces the stress of hospitalization and illness.

Some Tips for Visiting the Sick

- Wear an identification badge if provided.
- Read and respect isolation signs.
- Don mask, gown or gloves for protection when indicated.
- Observe health procedures, including frequent hand-washing.
- If you are not feeling well, try to visit another time.
- Be observant. Practice assessing situations at a glance.
- Read posted signs: HOH (hard-of-hearing), blind, NPO (*nil per os* or "nothing by mouth").
- If the door is closed, knock for permission to enter.
- If the bed curtains are drawn, do not enter without knocking.
- Return later if nurses or doctors are attending.
- Focus your attention on the patient.
- Identify yourself fully, explaining why you are there.
- Remember that the sick are the hosts. You are the guest.
- Quiet and ease are contagious. Be at peace.
- Stand or sit where the patient can see you easily.

- Do not lean or sit on the bed.

- Do not offer the patient food, cigarettes or drink. A drink of water may be appropriate if water is at bedside.

- Do not lift or assist the patient in moving.

- Limit your visit to an appropriate length of time.

- Avoid discussing cases similar to the patient's.

- Encourage patients to talk about how they *feel* emotionally rather than discussing how they look. Appearances are deceptive.

- Find the patient's emotional level and empathize.

- Do not impose personal mood or ideas on the patient.

- Do not judge the patient.

- Listen! Listen much more than you talk.

- After visiting, ask yourself, "Who knows more about whom?" You are to gather more information about the patient than he or she learns about you.

- Refer special needs to a nurse or the chaplain.

- Visit only designated patients, floors or areas assigned to you.

- Do not discuss patients with others in public areas.

- Hold all information in strict confidence.

- Do not criticize the hospital or personnel.

- When in doubt, *ask*! Questions regarding hospital policies or procedures are appreciated.

CHAPTER FOUR

Visiting Homes and Nursing Homes

D uring an orientation program for new hospital employees, a questionnaire regarding care of the elderly was distributed. Only one of the many questions related to pastoral care: "As people grow older, they feel closer to God: true or false?"

The only chaplain in the group, I thought quickly and checked "true." To the delight of the nurses with me, the chaplain was wrong. "False," the findings reveal. It seems that aging people grow closer in their relationship to God only if they have had throughout life an ongoing relationship with God that has enabled them to put sufferings into perspective. Such a relationship helps them to feel that God does not plague them with pain and adversity but is with them through difficult times and is the source of their joys.

People who grow closer to God as they age also have relationships with other people: people with whom they can share their struggles; people to whom they can reach out for support; people whom they can help in some small way; people who love them. In short, in order to grow closer to God throughout life, we need to be Church to one another: two or more gathered in Christ's name (see Matthew 18:20).

The need for ministry to the elderly is rising as the population ages. Medical science has succeeded in extending the lifespan in the United States. The challenge for ministry is to enable those who are living longer to find meaning in their added decades.

During the more active years of life, people gather with friends, family and coworkers to share life's pleasures and distresses. Home and work responsibilities occupy a large segment of each week. For many, worshiping with others is a source of strength and energy—both emotional and spiritual.

Loneliness and isolation are primary enemies of the elderly. As the years go on, friends and family move away or become involved in their own busy lives. Some die. Retirement comes; responsibilities at home are reduced. Social gatherings are fewer. Diminished hearing and sight may further narrow the world of the elderly. Physical limitations begin to make it difficult to attend church. They may begin to feel more and more alone. Those who feel forgotten or neglected by family and friends may also feel abandoned by God. Thus the experience of Church shrivels unless someone seeks to *be* Church with the elderly in nursing facilities or in their homes.

Most readers have succumbed at one time or another to the temptation to leap to the final chapter of a book to discover what happens at the end. Visiting the elderly offers the opportunity to read their stories from the concluding chapters backward to earlier years. As philosopher Søren Kierkegaard noted, life must be lived forward but can only be understood backward. As you talk with those whose lives fill many chapters, sharing their retrospective understanding of the events of their lives is a blessing.

Qualities to cultivate as you visit the elderly include: patience, willingness to spend time with them and to value lives that are less "productive," appreciation of the wisdom that comes with years, enjoyment of trips in memory to days gone by and love for the no-longer-young.

More than one visitor has complained of an older person's repetitious accounts of family and activities. Because the elderly's sphere of activity may be limited, it is natural that those nearby may hear more than they want about childhood memories and grandchildren and visits to the doctor. Yet the elderly possess an abundance of history and wisdom that is available to those who choose to listen. Visits from outside are usually welcome breaks in the routine of daily life. Because the elderly may move more slowly, think and speak more slowly and have much time to spend, you need to allow ample time to be present to them. A leisurely visit conveys the message that the person is important to you.

As with every patient you visit, avoid assumptions drawn from the age of the person. To speak loudly to an 85-year-old is to minimize her abilities; she may hear perfectly well. Quality visits begin by addressing each elderly patient or nursing home resident as an intelligent, capable adult. If you discover a hearing deficit, then turn up your volume a bit and slow your speech.

Sometimes you may suspect a computer error. That

was certainly my assumption when I read, "Nettie—age 107." As I looked into Nettie's room, I was even more certain that there was a mistake. She was an old woman, but 107? Not a chance! We began to chat at normal voice volume.

"Now I don't want you to think I'm here because I fell," Nellie declared, defending herself and her vitality. "I went into the bathroom at home the other night—I live by myself you know—and felt a little lightheaded so I just held onto the side of the tub and kind of lowered myself to the floor."

Nettie's heart had missed a couple of beats that night. The doctors were looking into the possibility of giving her a pacemaker to keep her heart beating regularly. "Then I'll be able to go back home!" she announced.

Nettie's daughter entered the room and the conversation. "Now, Mom, at your age it seems like a good time to look into a home where you can have a little extra attention. She's 107, you know," she said to me. So the computer hadn't lied! Nettie received her pacemaker (possibly the oldest pacemaker recipient in the world) and agreed to move into a nursing home. She celebrated her birthday number 111 in 1991. Her birthdays have become parish events at the church where she still worships each Sunday. She recently told a friend that she has to hold onto the pew in front to stand up now. Nellie remains a vivid reminder not to judge people and their capabilities by the number of years in their lives.

Evaluating the length of an individual's life by our standards is also risky. A man who was diagnosed with prostate cancer at seventy was not consoled by the young "grief girl" (as he named the social worker assigned to him) sent to counsel him after his diagnosis. She reminded him that he had had "a good long life." To a well-loved man of wisdom, inquisitive intellect and ample ability, seventy did not seem like a "long" life. Neither had he any intention of leaving this life just yet. He refused to see the "grief girl" again and years later lives on in good health, contributing much to the world.

To treat an aged or bedridden person as a child in speech or demeanor is to offend the dignity of that individual. Becky was horrified to hear a nursing-home aide ask her 92-year-old grandfather, "Does Henry have to go 'wee-wee' now?" Her grandparents had only recently moved to the nursing facility from the two-story home where they had lived for many decades. His present illness was his first serious bout with poor health. On her next visit Becky brought a photograph of her grandfather and grandmother at her wedding a few months earlier. She chose a positive, visual way to establish with the staff the dignity of the man who had so recently danced at her wedding.

Assure the people you visit that you accept them just as they are. If a mind seems a bit confused, take extra time to explain your mission. "Martha, it is perfectly OK that you didn't remember my name. I forget names too." You come to share a few moments of the day if that is their wish. As you do so, affirm the vitality that each person possesses; grieve with them their losses; offer hope for the future and the eternal.

Some Tips for Visiting Nursing Homes

Be consistent in visiting the elderly. A bond of friendship can be established if you visit a nursing home resident on a regular basis.

Establish rapport with the resident. Share a bit more of your own life and background than you might in a hospital visit. Knowing about where you live broadens the resident's limited physical world. Introducing your family to the resident through conversation puts new people in his or her life. You may discover links of common interest through conversation—a market you have both frequented, a church you attended, mutual acquaintances. This kind of linking partially places residents back into a world from which they may feel estranged. Even briefly sharing a *few* of your own aches and pains, if you have any, helps the resident feel a kinship of bodily discomfort.

Be pleasant but not overwhelmingly cheerful as you visit. Excessive cheer depresses those who find little to be cheerful about on a particular day.

Listen, listen, listen! Ask how things have been going for them for the last few days. (Going back a few days broadens residents' time frame.) If today happens to be a not-so-good day, they may benefit by telling you about what they did yesterday when they were more chipper. If today they feel more energetic than a few days ago, that also is a healthy reminder that "down" days are followed by "up" days. Hope springs from realizing that good days follow bad ones.

Inquire about personal concerns. This is not being nosy; it is being realistic. Family matters, financial worries, relationship concerns magnify in the minds of those who have fewer activities and outlets to balance the impact of problems. Those with whom they discussed matters in the past may be far away, deceased or unable to help at the present. Sharing concerns with an interested person lightens the burden.

Touch. Many who have hugged the elderly, held their hands, kissed them, patted them on the back and caressed them are gone from their lives. The human need for touch is well documented. Infants raised with all essentials of food, drink and cleanliness fail to thrive when deprived of human touch. That need does not vanish with passing years.

As I watched a senior citizen bowling league, one gesture became very obvious. After each bowler returned from bowling, all hands on the team reached out to brush palms, whether ten pins or none had fallen. The behavior expressed the need for human touch. The bowlers obliged each other by giving hands of acceptance again and again.

But remember that not all people like to be touched, especially by people whom they do not know well. Illness may leave others highly sensitive to touch. Allow the other person's actions to tell you about his need for touch. Begin slowly: Shaking hands is usually acceptable. Or lay your hand atop another's. Does the person seem to accept that touch? Or does she withdraw even a little? Does he respond by grasping your hand? Being observant enables you to provide the human touch the person needs.

George was ninety-one when he began to have difficulty with his hip replacement. Doctors finally determined that it would have to be replaced again if he were to have any mobility. The choice was to be George's. I asked him if he was going to choose another new hip. "Of course, I am! Do you think I want to be an invalid the rest of my life?" he retorted.

"I'm sure you wouldn't like that," I replied, laying my hand on his.

Immediately he grasped it tightly. That firm hold seemed to represent the grasp he longed to keep on life and on his independence.

"I can't tell you how long it's been since anyone held my hand," he murmured with glistening eyes and an impish smile.

Bring gifts. For those who have few visitors, small gifts blossom into treasures. A package of tissues, inexpensive greeting cards and a few stamps with which to remember others on special days, a prayer card, a flower or small plant—all these leave a visible remembrance of the visit after you are gone. The ultimate gift, however, is your presence.

Good-byes and Hellos

A recently retired pastor has decided to devote his retirement years to helping people say good-bye. In leaving his work and in moving from the church he had served for a number of years, he discovered the painful process of saying good-bye. Earlier transfers had not been so difficult because new opportunities were on the horizon. New challenges awaited. But when retirement came, the move involved a different kind of good-bye, one marked more heavily by loss. No new congregation waited to greet him. He could not anticipate new responsibilities to fill his days. This round of good-byes was saddened by the absence of hellos.

He realized that those who enter nursing homes face a sense of loss similar to his, though even more dramatic. His new goal is to accompany couples and individuals as they prepare to leave their homes for surroundings where their needs for medical care, housing and food can be better met. He helps them say good-bye to furnishings, neighbors and neighborhoods, houses or apartments, and the memories those aspects of their past hold for them. He reflects with them as they choose what to take with them into their new homes.

For those who have lived in familiar, secure surroundings for many years, meeting new neighbors and adapting to new surroundings and activities can be difficult. To meet this challenge those who move must learn to say hello again. They must greet new people who are potential friends, find new activities which can provide life-giving interests, adjust to new surroundings which in time will become home—in a different sense from the old one, but still home.

You can facilitate good-byes and hellos. As you visit nursing homes, listen as residents mourn their loss of mobility, of the family car and the family homestead. Rejoice with them when they make friends with whom they can play favorite card games or swap stories.

Your presence can assure residents that the Church and their God have not said good-bye to them during the transition. Bringing Communion and prayer provides assurance of God's continued care and presence. One nursing home volunteer discovered that her visiting time could be profitably spent by gathering the people she was sent to visit into a Bible study group. Some who had lived alone for many years were initially shy. Within a short time these former strangers were saying friendly hellos to each other through their Scripture study. Your hellos on behalf of the Church serve as a constant reminder of God's love for the elderly.

You will meet a diversity of individuals in nursing homes. Residing in a nursing facility does not reduce people to a single level of interests, abilities and capabilities. Some residents will be mentally alert, physically active and eager for conversation and companionship. Others may be beyond cognitive communication. Pastoral care visits affirm the value of lives lived at various levels of human activity and awareness.

Shut In and Shut Out

Shut-ins are often shut out of mainstream community activity. Respiratory problems, immobility, overwhelming fear of crowds, frailness of body, dependence on medical equipment—these are but a few of the captors that hold people hostage in their homes. Shut-ins are not necessarily elderly; these afflictions can attack people of any age. Many who are physically confined are not mental shut-ins. They maintain connections with the world through phone conversations, writing, reading and television. Some work at their vocations from their homes.

Your visit will be guided by the principles for hospital visitation or nursing home calls modified to meet the specific needs of the shut-in you visit. Your visit provides what other activities cannot: caring personal presence. Those who visit bring a segment of the world to a person who cannot venture into the world. You bring *Church*, that gathering of two or more in the name of Jesus, to one who is unable to attend worship services. As a pastoral care visitor you bring your own personal charisma: your smile, your touch, your compassion conveyed face-to-face.

Your visit is not the visit of an individual. You come in the name of the Church; your visit represents the concern of many. Your visit enables *communion*, union with the Body of Christ.

CHAPTER FIVE

Caring for the Caregivers

As you pass through the corridors of health-care facilities, you come in contact with a uniquely gifted group of people: the caregivers. Doctors, nurses, aides, transporters, clerks, maintenance staff— many people enter health care because of genuine compassion for the sick.

Theirs is not an easy lot. Many require lengthy and ongoing education to maintain their competence. Understaffing may structure long and difficult shifts. Patients reacting to the stress of illness may greet their efforts with less-than-appreciative attitudes. Caregivers must cope with the challenges of their professions while bearing the usual responsibilities of family life. And, while most of their patients go back to daily life healed or healing, many staff members witness patients' ongoing struggles with chronic disease, progressive disability or mortal illness. To even the most professional health-care provider, these factors spell stress.

Be aware of the needs of these dedicated men and women. Seek opportunities to affirm their work, reduce their tensions and lift their spirits. As you observe a nurse caring for a contentious individual, you note her cheerful disposition does not falter when confronted by her cranky patient's displeasure. Inquiring how she maintains such a pleasant outlook provides two benefits: You affirm the positive nature of her care and you have the opportunity to learn how another person copes with testy individuals.

A visitor who observes special caring can mention the good work of the one whose work exceeds the job description. Susan, a very intuitive nurse, has the ability to understand the source of her patient's aggravation. "You're feeling grouchy today because the doctor hasn't discharged you. You're afraid you'll miss that grandson's wedding." The patient, who had complained about everything from her food to the color of the draperies, softened. "You're right. I get so angry when there's nothing I can do to change things." The patient's day improved when she could admit to what was bothering her and the nurse's work eased with her patient's improved attitude. Susan's pride in her work soared when the pastoral visitor, who had overheard the conversation, later commented on her perception of the patient's frustration.

Maria's job is to clean the rooms in a children's hospital. She chats with the children and their parents as she works. So comforting is her approach that she is often privy to information that is pertinent to the patients' care. In her gentle way she will share her finding with the staff members who provide direct patient care. "Did you know that Jennifer misses her pet, Roughy, a whole lot?" And a picture of Roughy appeared in the girl's room.

Another maintenance worker beamed when a

pastoral care visitor mentioned the extraordinary cleaning she gave each room. "Well, I look at it this way," she explained. "There are nurses who take care of the patients and there are people to take care of the rooms. I'm kind of the room nurse. Together we help people get well." Noticing excellence in work and commenting to the person involved raises the self-esteem of caregivers.

Not all caregivers are able to give TLC at all times. A particular aide grumbled and growled at patients and nurses alike. The weekly pastoral care visitor in the hospital wondered what her life was like outside the hospital walls. And so he asked, "What do you do for fun and relaxation when you go home?"

"Do?" the aide snapped. "The same thing I do here! Take care of my mother." As they talked about the burden of doing the same work virtually twenty-four hours a day, he discovered that her mother had given her little love over her lifetime; the mother's alcoholism had destroyed their relationship. Caring for a cantankerous mother who had given her little besides life had created a bitter woman. At the conclusion of their conversation, the visitor noted the first smile he had ever seen on the aide's face. The burden was not removed, but it was lightened by sharing and understanding.

To provide support for caregivers without interfering with patient care is important. You can join them as they walk to a patient's room or to the nursing station. If you sense the time is not fitting for the conversation you have initiated, a friendly, "I'll catch up with you another time. I see you're really busy today," will disengage you.

Caring for Families

Family members or friends often need assurance that it is perfectly OK to take care of themselves. They may be torn between their need to be at the hospital and the need to maintain their daily lives. Frustration and guilt may arise as they attempt to resolve this conflict. When you have a chance out of a patient's earshot, ask how the hospitalization of a relative affects their lives. This offers an opportunity for them to speak honestly about the challenges of daily schedules. The patient needs healthy caregivers, not people stressed to the point of being vulnerable to sickness themselves.

Family visitors may be overwhelmed by medical equipment. Because you do not represent the medical profession, they may feel less foolish admitting to you that they do not understand the paraphernalia and procedures. As an intermediary, you can ask the nurse to explain the patient's care and equipment. Knowledge reduces apprehension.

When a patient returns home, primary care may fall on a spouse or an adult child. As the release date nears, look for opportunities to speak with that person away from the patient's room to discuss feelings about the person's return home. Hospitalization may spell freedom from caring for an individual twenty-four hours a day—a real relief for the caregiver. Yet experiencing that relief can trigger guilt. On the one hand, a caregiver wants the patient to be discharged. At the same time, the patient's return home will increase the workload. Financial concerns can also be entwined with the mixed emotions. Once again, your empathetic listening skills can permit the person to unload some of that guilt.

Primary caregivers may also be concerned that they will not be able to provide the care their loved one needs upon release from the hospital. Social service workers and nursing staff are ultimately responsible for helping the caregiver resolve this problem. In the meantime you can provide the gift of a listening ear. The opportunity to discuss fears relieves stress.

Parents of sick or injured children encounter particular problems in dealing with hospitalization. The illness may cause the parent to question parenting skills: "Should I have...?" or "If I had only..." cause unease and tension. Depending on the seriousness of the child's condition, the parent can experience full-blown guilt or depression.

Alex had driven only a couple of blocks without checking six-year-old Molly's seat belt when their car was hit broadside by a truck that had run a red light. He needed to tell many people how badly he felt about his negligence. Each confession was like peeling a layer away from the onion of his guilt. When Molly finally was able to tell him, "It's OK, Daddy; you didn't mean to have an accident and I should have buckled my seat belt," Alex had reached the point where he could forgive himself. In the process many visitors had heard his confession with compassion—and without telling him that he "shouldn't feel that way."

Mary Ellen's teenage son, Ryan, arrived home from basketball practice very sick and went straight to bed. He complained of severe stomach pains. His symptoms matched a flu that several of Mary Ellen's friends had complained of and she treated Ryan accordingly. Many hours later she became alarmed that he seemed to be getting worse rather than better. By the time Ryan was admitted to the hospital with a ruptured appendix, his very life was endangered. Mary Ellen's anguish over her misdiagnosis was discovered by a parish visitor who noted that Mary Ellen looked almost as sick as Ryan. In the conversation that followed Mary Ellen was able to express the guilt that was gnawing within her.

The bedside vigil is often a parent's way of coping with a child's illness or injury. Mrs. Gilman told a volunteer that she had not left her daughter's side since she had been admitted to the hospital. The volunteer asked what Mrs. Gilman would be doing on such a beautiful spring day if Sarah were not in the hospital. With a smile, the mother responded that she would be working in her garden. The volunteer invited Sarah's mom to walk with her in a garden area near the hospital. The two walked and talked about gardens and flowers, about spring and life and children. As they returned to the hospital, the volunteer thought Mrs. Gilman looked years younger. The talk and walk in the sunshine had given her a new perspective on life. Sarah would benefit from her mom's renewal as well.

Parents must provide love and care for other children at home as well as for the hospitalized child. Maintaining home life and work schedules at near-normal levels taxes the limits of most families. The pastoral care visitor cannot erase these factors for a family. But awareness of potential stressors will enable the visitor to initiate meaningful conversation with parents.

Caring for Yourself

Take care of yourself, too. You have shared another's burden. You have entered into confidentialities. You have listened to emotions ranging from anger at God to joy in knowing God. You have seen life torn by illness or enriched by its presence. In a variety of ways you have taken on an enormous amount of emotional and spiritual baggage.

This baggage becomes a part of *your* life's journey. How you process your visit determines how it will affect your life and your ministry. What you learn from each visit will guide and shape your ministry to the sick and their families. Feelings and emotions that are not dealt with will weigh you down. Unrecognized feelings fuel emotional burnout in ministry to the sick.

Caring for her mother through her last days inspired Mary to undertake a practicum in pastoral care skills. But Mary was concerned that she might mentally take patients and their problems home with her. She knew it was essential to herself and to those she visited to separate herself emotionally and spiritually at the end of a visiting day. While recognizing that her sensitive nature was a gift to this ministry, Mary knew it could also cause burnout. So she devised a strategy for follow-up after pastoral care visits.

On her drive home from the hospital, Mary allows her mind to return to the patients she has visited. As she revisits in thought, she first asks herself, "What did I like about what I did?" Thus she affirms herself and her work. She knows that she has much to share with the sick.

She also knows that she wants to grow in her

ministry, to learn new skills and approaches, so she asks herself, "What could I have done differently?" She explores alternatives even when she believes the way she handled a situation initially was the best choice. Thus she stores away a new plan that may someday apply to another patient.

In areas where she was not totally satisfied and for which she has not found alternatives, she asks, "Who can help me with this?" She may turn to her pastor, her supervisor or the nursing staff.

Before retiring for the night, Mary proceeds with a further step in processing the day. Sometimes she enters feelings and events of the day in her journal in her own free style. Other times she follows a guided form to review her work. The form contains the following questions:

- What did I allow myself to learn about me?
- What did I allow myself to learn about patients and their families?
- What did I allow myself to learn about sickness and health?
- What did I allow myself to learn about my theology?
- Where is God in this?

(Notice the key word *allow*. Each of us has many opportunities for learning in any given day. We need to give ourselves *permission* to learn and to be changed by those experiences. The challenge is to see how to learn and grow in negative experiences as well as positive ones.)

Finally, to bring closure to the process of divesting herself from patient care, Mary prays for her patients. Knowing she has done what she was called to do and was able to do, she entrusts them to God, releasing herself to a peaceful evening and night.

This process may seem lengthy. Actually, it can be done in a relatively brief time. It is well worth the effort. Time spent processing the day's events is invaluable in preventing that insidious malady called burnout, which results when others' burdens so fill your emotional and spiritual space that you bog down, your energy flags, your faith quavers and your work falters.

Beware of the tendency of ministry to the sick to draw you into a vortex. Take time for yourself. Laugh, play, pray, love, gather vitality into yourself. You will then have joy and peace, energy and life to share through your presence.

CHAPTER SIX

Prayers and Blessings

Whenever in the writing of this book I reached an impasse, a mental block, a dry spell, I returned to this section to pray and write prayers. The message this seems to bring is that at any point in our ministry where staleness, doubt, lack of confidence, fatigue creep into our effectiveness, prayer is the only answer.

Morning and Evening Prayers

MORNING OFFERING

Each new day, Lord,
is an unknown adventure.

We ask that this day bring
no surprise that with your help we cannot handle,
no difficulty that with your patience we cannot
    subdue,
no pain that with your courage we cannot bear.

We ask, Lord,
for the adventure of seeking you in new places
within ourselves and in others,
of finding you in adversity
through which you will lead us to triumph. Amen.

MORNING PRAYER

O Lord, as this day begins,
we praise you and thank you
for whatever is in store for us.

We trust in your grace to endure the difficult
and to rejoice in the blessings.

Use N. to touch the lives of those who care for
    her/him
with your gifts of peace, love and understanding.
Amen.

FOR THE RECOVERING

Thank you, God, that today N. experiences your
    healing power.
The journey through illness is not over, but healing
    has begun.
We are grateful that past days are but memories.
We ask for faith to live today trusting in your Spirit.
We place the hope of tomorrow in your hands. Amen.

PRAYER OF PRAISE

Praised be God for bringing me to this place.
You know, God, that I do not want to be here.
I want to be home, living my everyday life.
But because I am sick I will praise you for placing me
where I can be cared for by those who understand
this human body
which you created for me
in my mother's womb.

Praise you and thank you for each person
who is sent to care for me.
Help them and help me
to live this day in your love. Amen.

IN THANKSGIVING FOR LIFE

Alleluia, Lord, we are alive!
We live in you and you in us.
With this knowledge the problems of today
can be met one at a time.
Your life in us brings courage to live
with hope and faith and love.

We rejoice in the assurance
that at the dawn of the day
when our physical life ends,
your life will continue in our spirits
for eternity.
Alleluia, Lord, we are alive. Amen.

THE DIVINE GUARDIAN

I lift up my eyes toward the mountains;
    whence shall help come to me?
My help is from the LORD,
    who made heaven and earth.

May he not suffer your foot to slip;
    may he slumber not who guards you:
Indeed he neither slumbers nor sleeps,
    the guardian of Israel.

The LORD is your guardian; the LORD is your shade;
    he is beside you at your right hand.
The sun shall not harm you by day,
    nor the moon by night.

The LORD will guard you from all evil;
    he will guard your life.
The LORD will guard your coming and your going,
    both now and forever. (Psalm 121:1-4)

THE GREATNESS OF GOD

I will extol you, O my God and King,
    and I will bless your name forever and ever.
Every day will I bless you,
    and I will praise your name forever and ever.
Great is the LORD and highly to be praised;
    his greatness is unsearchable. (Psalm 145:1-3)

DOXOLOGY

Glory be to the Father
and to the Son
and to the Holy Spirit,
As it was in the beginning,
is now and ever shall be
world without end. Amen.

COME, HOLY SPIRIT

Come, Holy Spirit, come!
And from your celestial home
Shed a ray of light divine!

Come, Father of the poor!
Come, source of all our store!
Come, within our bosoms shine!

You, of comforters the best;
You, the soul's most welcome guest;
Sweet refreshment here below;

In our labor, rest most sweet;
Grateful coolness in the heat,
Solace in the midst of woe....

Heal our wounds, our strength renew;
On our dryness pour thy dew;
Wash the stains of guilt away:

Bend the stubborn heart and will;
Melt the frozen, warm the chill;
Guide the steps that go astray.
(Sequence for Pentecost)

Thank you, Lord,
for another day of life.

Thank you for a day
which brought nothing you and I together
were not able to handle.

Thank you for the prospect of a night of rest
knowing you will be with me until the dawn. Amen.

FOR REST

Loving God, you who give rest to the weary, grant N.
a night of peaceful sleep.
May this time of rest be a time of renewal of body,
mind and spirit.
May he/she awaken with an awareness of your loving
presence.
May morning bring the gift of praise. Amen.

Prayers for Times of Pain, Fear and Suffering

JESUS' INVITATION

Come to me, all you who labor and are burdened, and I will give you rest. Take my yoke upon you and learn from me, for I am meek and humble of heart; and you will find rest for yourselves. (Matthew 11:28-29)

IN TIME OF FEAR

Where are you, Jesus, when I need you?
Fear and pain have swept my life into a whirlpool
   of panic.
Night is endless, yet day brings little peace.
I call your name. Please answer me.
I need reassurance in the fog of my fright.
Where are you, Jesus, when I need you?
Ah, you are here—within me.
With me you suffer, too.
Yes, you are here—beside me
   in the love of others,
   in the care of the nurses,
   in the wisdom of doctors,
   in the prayer of the person who cleans this room.
You are here, Jesus, when I need you! Amen.

GOD'S PLAN

For I know well the plans I have in mind for you, says the LORD, plans for your welfare, not for woe! plans to give you a future full of hope. (Jeremiah 29:11)

ST. TERESA'S BOOKMARK

Let nothing disturb you,
nothing affright you.
All things are passing;
God never changes.
Patient endurance attains to all things.
Whoever possesses God is wanting in nothing;
God alone suffices.

THE DIVINE SHEPHERD

The LORD is my shepherd; I shall not want.
   In verdant pastures he gives me repose;
Beside restful waters he leads me;
   he refreshes my soul.
He guides me in right paths
   for his name's sake.
Even though I walk in the dark valley
   I fear no evil; for you are at my side
With your rod and your staff
   that give me courage.

You spread the table before me
   in the sight of my foes;
You anoint my head with oil;
   my cup overflows.
Only goodness and kindness follow me
   all the days of my life;
And I shall dwell in the house of the LORD
   for years to come. (Psalm 23)

Hear, O God, my cry;
  listen to my prayer!
From the earth's end I call to you
  as my heart grows faint. (Psalm 61:1-2)

I JUST CAN'T PRAY

I want to pray, Lord Jesus, but I just can't right now.
My fear and anger at being sick seem to take my
  power to pray away.
I want to come to you with words that soar.
Instead my heart shouts, "No more!"
No more pain and no more doubt.
Could it be this is what prayer's about—
Offering you my pain and fear,
not just words I choose for you to hear?
Now I seem to understand.
Though I thought I couldn't pray,
Still your Spirit speaks for me this day. Amen.

DO NOT FEAR

Do not fear what may happen tomorrow. The same
loving Father who cares for you today will care for you
tomorrow and every day. Either he will shield you
from suffering or he will give you unfailing strength to
bear it. Be at peace, then, and put aside all anxious
thoughts and imaginings. (St. Francis de Sales)

The LORD is my light and my salvation;
  whom should I fear?
The LORD is my life's refuge;
  of whom should I be afraid?
When evildoers come at me
  to devour my flesh,
My foes and my enemies
  themselves stumble and fall.
Though an army encamp against me,
  my heart will not fear;
Though war be waged upon me,
  even then will I trust.

One thing I ask of the LORD;
  this I seek:
To dwell in the house of the LORD
  all the days of my life,
That I may gaze on the loveliness of the LORD
  and contemplate his temple.
For he will hide me in his abode
  in the day of trouble;
He will conceal me in the shelter of his tent,
  he will set me high upon a rock.
Even now my head is held high
  above my enemies on every side.
And I will offer in his tent
  sacrifices with shouts of gladness;
I will sing and chant praise to the LORD. (Psalm 27)

Father,
I abandon myself into your hands;
do with me what you will.
Whatever you may do, I thank you;
I am ready for all; I accept all.
Let only your will be done in me
and in all your creatures—
I wish no more than this, O Lord.

Into your hands I commend my soul;
I offer it to you with all the love of my heart,
for I love you, Lord,
and so need to give myself,
to surrender myself into your hands
without reserve and with boundless confidence.
For you are my Father. (Charles de Foucauld)

ANTICIPATING SURGERY

Loving God, you who give comfort to the weary and
frightened,
give N. peace and courage as the time of surgery
approaches.
Reassure her/him of your presence.
Creator God, you who designed N.'s very being,
may your Spirit fill the medical staff with your wisdom
and knowledge.
Merciful God, provide your strength where N.'s own
strength is insufficient.
Call N. to surrender herself/himself into your care
this day. Amen.

BEFORE SURGERY

God of compassion,
our human weakness lays claim to your strength.

We pray that through the skills of surgeons and
nurses your healing gifts may be granted to N.

May your servant respond to your healing will
and be reunited with us at your altar of praise.
(*Pastoral Care of the Sick*, #159)

FOR HEALING

Lord Jesus,
you know how I feel today,
my secret fears and pains.
I pray for healing
in whatever way
you know will help me.
I trust in your power.
You proclaimed God's reign
by curing the sick,
comforting and strengthening
those who were sad,
and giving new freedom
to all who accepted you.
Guide those who help
in your healing work:
doctors, nurses, chaplains
and all who extend care.
Together we do the work
of your Father.

We pray in your Spirit,
Lord Jesus. Amen.
(Franciscan Vocation Office Prayer Card)

FOR THE AGED

Merciful God, you who are without age,
Look upon your servant N. with love.
Help N. to accept the changes of life
   that come with an abundance of years.
Give her/him courage to live this day in harmony
   with you.
As bodily strength wanes, grant N. increasing faith.
As eyesight dims, enable her/him to see your
presence.
As hearing fails, let her/him attend to your word.
As days grow long, give N. patience to wait upon you.
Amen.

GOD'S COMING

Strengthen the hands that are feeble,
   make firm the knees that are weak,
Say to those whose hearts are frightened:
   Be strong, fear not!
Here is your God,
   he comes with vindication;
With divine recompense
   he comes to save you.
Then will the eyes of the blind be opened,
   the ears of the deaf be cleared;
Then will the lame leap like a stag,

then the tongue of the dumb will sing.

...Those whom the LORD has ransomed will return
   and enter Zion singing,
   crowned with everlasting joy;
They will meet with joy and gladness,
   sorrow and mourning will flee. (Isaiah 35:3-6a, 10)

FOR THE DYING

What will separate us from the love of Christ? Will
anguish, or distress, or persecution, or famine, or
nakedness, or peril or the sword? As it is written:

"For your sake we are being slain all the day;
   we are looked upon as sheep to be slaughtered."

No, in all these things we conquer overwhelmingly
through him who loved us. For I am convinced that
neither death, nor life, nor angels, nor principalities,
nor present things, nor future things, nor powers, nor
height, nor depth, nor any other creature will be able
to separate us from the love of God in Christ Jesus our
Lord. (Romans 8:35-39)

FOR THE GRIEVING

[God] will wipe every tear from their eyes, and there
shall be no more death or mourning, wailing or pain,
[for] the old order has passed away. (Revelation 21:4)

AT DEATH

Sister Death,
Oh, kind and tender death,
Gently come to still the breath,
Praise the Father! Glory! Praise!
Welcome this loved one today
For Christ our Lord has shown the way.
Oh, praise and glory! Glory! Praise!
(Inspired by the Canticle of St. Francis)

CANTICLE OF SIMEON

Now, Master, you may let your servant go
    in peace, according to your word,
for my eyes have seen your salvation,
    which you prepared in sight of all the peoples,
a light for revelation to the Gentiles,
    and glory for your people Israel. (Luke 2:29-32)

THE HOPE

I consider that the sufferings of this present time are
as nothing compared with the glory to be revealed for
us. (Romans 8:18)

Oh, Lord, receive the spirit of N., your child.
Free him/her from the pain and struggle of this life.
Give N.'s family and friends faith and strength to
release him/her to your loving care.
May the saints and angels welcome him/her into the
life that has no end. Amen.

FOR THE CAREGIVER

Lord, we pray for the staff of this hospital today.
To those who are job-weary, give a new vision of their
work's value.
To those who are anxious in their work, provide your
peace.
May those who find satisfaction in their occupation
rejoice.
Inspire each individual to learn something new today
about their work, their patients and themselves.
In doing this may they come to know you more
deeply. Amen.

FOR MEDICAL PERSONNEL

Bless, O Lord, those whom you have given the art of
physical healing, the prevention of disease and the
soothing of pain. May your Spirit strengthen their
days, enlighten their minds and quicken their spirits
of compassion and caring. May they become
cocreators with you of the broken bodies entrusted to
their care. Amen.

Heavenly Father, we come to you seeking peace of mind for the family and friends who are concerned about N. May they find comfort in each other and in the knowledge that N. is in your care. Cast out fear and fill their hearts with faith and love. Amen.

Sacramental Moments

AT COMMUNION

I am the bread of life; whoever comes to me will never hunger, and whoever believes in me will never thirst....For this is the will of my Father, that everyone who sees the Son and believes in him may have eternal life, and I shall raise him [on] the last day....I am the living bread that came down from heaven; whoever eats this bread will live forever; and the bread that I will give is my flesh for the life of the world. (John 6:35b, 40, 51)

COMMUNION OF THE SICK IN ORDINARY CIRCUMSTANCES

Eucharistic Minister: The peace of the Lord be with you always.

Response: And also with you.

E.M.: My brothers and sisters, to prepare ourselves for this celebration, let us call to mind our sins.

(Pause)

Lord Jesus, you healed the sick:
Lord, have mercy.

R.: Lord, have mercy.

E.M.: Lord Jesus, you forgave sinners:
Christ, have mercy.

R.: Christ, have mercy.

E.M.: Lord Jesus, you give us yourself to heal us and
bring us strength:
Lord, have mercy.

R.: Lord, have mercy.

Or:

All: I confess to almighty God,
and to you, my brothers and sisters,
that I have sinned through my own fault
in my thoughts and in my words,
in what I have done,
and in what I have failed to do;
and I ask blessed Mary, ever virgin,
all the angels and saints,
and you, my brothers and sisters,
to pray for me to the Lord our God.

E.M.: May almighty God have mercy on us,
forgive us our sins,
and bring us to everlasting life.

R.: Amen.

E.M.: A reading from the holy Gospel according to John:

Jesus says:
"I am the way, and the truth, and the life;
no one comes to the Father but through me."
(John 6:51)

This is the Gospel of the Lord.

Eucharistic Minister: Now let us pray as Christ the Lord has taught us:

All: Our Father....

E.M. (showing the Blessed Sacrament): This is the bread of life.
Taste and see that the Lord is good.

All: Lord, I am not worthy to receive you,
but only say the word and I shall be healed.

E.M.: The body of Christ.

R.: Amen.

E.M. (if offering both species): The blood of Christ.

R.: Amen.

(Silent prayer.)

E.M.: All-powerful and ever-living God,
may the body and blood of Christ your Son
be for our brother/sister N.
a lasting remedy for body and soul.
We ask this through Christ our Lord.
Amen. (*Pastoral Care of the Sick*, #81-90)

Eucharistic Minister: How holy this feast
   in which Christ is our food:
   his passion is recalled;
   grace fills our hearts;
   and we receive a pledge of the glory to come.

   The peace of the Lord be with you always.

Response: And also with you.

E.M.: Jesus taught us to call God our Father, and so
   we have the courage to say:

All: Our Father....

E.M.: This is the Lamb of God who takes away the
   sins of the world. Happy are those who hunger and
   thirst, for they shall be satisfied.

R.: Lord, I am not worthy to receive you,
   but only say the word and I shall be healed.

E.M.: The body of Christ.

R.: Amen.

E.M.: Let us pray.

   All powerful and ever-living God,
   may the body and blood of Christ your Son
   be for our brothers and sisters
   a lasting remedy for body and soul.
   (*Pastoral Care of the Sick*, #92-95)

As we come together, we claim your promise, Lord, that where two or more gather in your name, you are present. We come to you more perfectly when we are forgiven for whatever stands between us. We ask you to help call to mind whatever separates us from your love and grant us your forgiveness.

Pause.

Forgiven, we come with the prayer you taught your disciples as we pray together, "Our Father...."

PRAYER AFTER COMMUNION

Lord Jesus, we praise you and thank you for choosing to sacrifice your body so that our bodies might share your health, hope, happiness and, someday, life everlasting. We thank you for your Spirit whom you send to dwell in us, bringing us peace, comfort and joy. Lord, may your Spirit fill us with your gifts now and all the days of our life. We pray in the name of the Father, the Son and the Holy Spirit. Amen.

ANOINTING

Is anyone among you suffering? He should pray. Is anyone in good spirits? He should sing praise. Is anyone among you sick? He should summon the presbyters of the church, and they should pray over him and anoint [him] with oil in the name of the Lord, and the prayer of faith will save the sick person, and the Lord will raise him up. If he has committed any sins, he will be forgiven.

Therefore, confess your sins to one another and pray for one another, that you may be healed. The fervent prayer of a righteous person is very powerful. (James 5:13-16)

ACT OF CONTRITION

O my God, I am heartily sorry
for having offended you,
and I detest all my sins,
because of your just punishments,
but most of all because they offend you, my God,
who are all-good and deserving of all love.
I firmly resolve,
with the help of your grace,
to sin no more
and to avoid the occasions of sin.

Blessings

1) May God bless us this day with the assurance of his presence, the power of his healing in its many and varied forms, and the knowledge of his deep and abiding love for us. Amen.

2) May God bless us with peace to calm our fears, strength to support our weakness, faith to drive away our despair, love to fill our loneliness and hope to conquer doubt. Amen.

3) Blessed is the man who perseveres in temptation, for when he has been proved he will receive the crown of life that [God] promised to those who love him (James 1:12).

4) "Peace I leave with you; my peace I give to you. Not as the world gives do I give it to you" (John 14:27).

5) May the God of compassion hold us in the palm of his hand when we feel weary and alone in our suffering. May ours be the look of compassion and the touch of comfort to those who reach out to us in their need. May the blessing of compassion be with us.

6) May the God of peace fill us with calm. May our pounding fears and anguish be stilled by the comfort of the Holy Spirit. May our peace flow to those near us who are troubled by doubt. May the blessing of peace be with us.

7) May the God of love immerse us in the divine mercy.
May the spark of the Spirit of love ignite us and those
around us, enabling fires of faith and hope to engulf
our days. May the blessing of love empower our life.
Amen.

Minister: Our help is in the name of the Lord.

All: Who made heaven and earth.

*One of those present or the pastoral minister reads a text
from Sacred Scripture:*

Blessed be the God and Father of our Lord Jesus
Christ, the Father of compassion and God of all
encouragement, who encourages us in our every
affliction, so that we may be able to encourage those
who are in any affliction with the encouragement with
which we ourselves are encouraged by God. (2
Corinthians 1:3-4)

Or,

Jesus said: "Come to me, all you who labor and are
burdened, and I will give you rest. Take my yoke upon
you and learn from me, for I am meek and humble of
heart; and you will find rest for yourselves."
(Matthew 11:28-29)

*As circumstances suggest, a minister who is a priest or
deacon may lay hands on the sick person while saying the
prayer of blessing; a lay minister may trace the sign of the
cross on the sick person's forehead while saying the prayer.*

Lord and Father, almighty and eternal God,
by your blessing you give us strength and support
    in our frailty:
turn with kindness toward your servant, N.
Free him/her from all illness and restore him/her to
    health,
so that in the sure knowledge of your goodness
he/she will gratefully bless your holy name.

We ask this through Christ our Lord.

All: Amen. (*The Revised Book of Blessings*, #403-405)

SHORT FORMULARY

*As circumstances suggest, a priest or deacon may use the
following short blessing formulary.*

Minister: May he who alone is Lord and Redeemer
    bless + you, N.

May he give health to your body
and holiness to your soul.

May he bring you safely to eternal life.

All: Amen. (*Book of Blessings*, #406)

May God bless you with faith to quiet the fear of your hearts. May he give you courage to face the adversity of this time. May he strengthen you in love that grows through difficulties.

May God grant you grace to praise him in all this day's events. Amen.

FOR STAFF

May God bless you with wisdom for your decisions and the humility to recognize their Source.

May God give you compassion for your patients and his love, from which it springs.

May God grant you strength for this day's work and the will to rest in him when the day is done. Amen.

Other Resources

Books

Bolton, Robert. *People Skills*. Englewood Cliffs, N.J.: Prentice-Hall, 1979.

Bombeck, Erma. *I Want to Grow Hair, I Want to Grow Up, I Want to Go to Boise*. New York, N.Y.: Harper & Row, 1989.

Book of Blessings. Collegeville, Minn. The Liturgical Press, 1989.

Champlin, Rev. Joseph M. *Together by Your Side: A Book for Comforting the Sick and Dying*. Notre Dame, Ind.: Ave Maria Press, 1982.

Coan, Alphonse, O.F.M. *Prayer Book*. Chicago, Ill.: Franciscan Herald Press, 1974.

Cousins, Norman. *Anatomy of an Illness as Perceived by the Patient*. Boston: G. K. Hall, 1979.

_____. *Head First: The Biology of Hope*. New York, N.Y.: E. P. Dutton, 1989.

Egan, Gerard. *The Skilled Helper*. Monterey, Calif.: Brooks/Cole Publishing, 1982.

Fischer, Kathleen. *Winter Grace: Spirituality for the Later Years.* New York, N.Y.: Paulist Press, 1985.

Galipeau, Steven A. *Transforming Body and Soul: Therapeutic Wisdom in the Gospel Healing Stories.* Mahwah, N.J.: Paulist Press, 1990.

Hart, Thomas N. *The Art of Christian Listening.* New York, N.Y.: Paulist Press, 1980.

Kubler-Ross, Elisabeth. *On Death and Dying.* New York, N.Y.: Macmillan, 1969.

_____. *Questions and Answers on Death and Dying.* New York, N.Y.: Macmillan Publishing Co., 1974.

Lord, I Am Not Worthy. Chicago, Ill.: Liturgy Training Publications, 1983.

MacNutt, Francis. *Healing.* Notre Dame, Ind.: Ave Maria, 1974.

Normile, Patti. "When Your Child Is in the Hospital." St. Meinrad, Ind.: Abbey Press, 1990.

Nouwen, Henri J. M. *The Wounded Healer.* Garden City, N.Y.: Doubleday, 1972.

_____. *Creative Ministry.* Garden City, N.Y.: Doubleday & Co., 1971.

Peck, Scott M. *The Road Less Traveled.* New York, N.Y.: Simon & Schuster, 1978.

Powell, John. *Why Am I Afraid to Tell You Who I Am?* Chicago, Ill.: Argus Communications, 1969.

Prayers of the Sick. Chicago, Ill.: Liturgy Training Publications, 1981.

Richstatter, Rev. Thomas, O.F.M. *Would You Like to Be Anointed?* Cincinnati, Ohio: St. Anthony Messenger Press, 1987.

Shlemon, Barbara. *Healing Prayer.* Notre Dame, Ind.: Ave Maria Press, 1976.

Siegel, Bernie, M.D. *Love, Medicine and Miracles.* New York, N.Y.: Harper & Row, 1986.

Sing, Susan Saint. *Living With Sickness.* Cincinnati, Ohio: St. Anthony Messenger Press, 1987.

_____. *Peace, Love and Healing.* New York, N.Y.: Harper & Row, 1989.

The Rite of Anointing and Pastoral Care of the Sick. English Translation, International Committee on English in the Liturgy, Inc., 1973.

Audiotapes

Bryer, James W., Jr. *Becoming a Skilled Helper.* Kansas City, Mo.: National Catholic Reporter Publishing, 1985.

Guntzelman, Joan. *In Their Shoes.* Kansas City, Mo.: National Catholic Reporter Publishing, 1988.

Sing, Susan Saint with Murray Bodo, O.F.M. *The Desert Speaks: A Journey of Prayer for the Discouraged.* Cincinnati, Ohio: St. Anthony Messenger Press, 1983.

Turpin, Joanne. *The Healing Mysteries.* Cincinnati, Ohio: St. Anthony Messenger Press, 1984.